IF YOU DON'T FEED THE TEACHERS THEY EAT THE STUDENTS!

A Guide to Success for Administrators and Teachers

by Neila A. Connors, Ph.D.

Incentive Publications
Nashville, Tennessee

"Some peoples' food always tastes better than others,
even if they are cooking the same dish . . . because one person has
much more life in them—more fire, more vitality, more guts than others."
— Rosa Lewis, British Hotelier

Cover by Geoffrey Brittingham and Marta Drayton
Edited by Jennifer J. Streams and Angela Reiner

Library of Congress Card Number: 00-107562
ISBN 0-86530-457-2

PRINTED IN THE UNITED STATES OF AMERICA
www.incentivepublications.com

Dedication:

This book is dedicated to the memory of Guy Bennett, a wonderful human being and outstanding administrator.

I first met Guy in 1983, during my internship to his school in Venice, Florida, while researching his advisory program for my dissertation. Upon entering his school, my first thoughts centered around the friendly, warm, and inviting atmosphere. After a day of observations, I asked Guy what his secret was to creating a friendly and inviting climate. Guy replied, "I have two beliefs. My first is that to be successful you must be a **cheerleader-leader**. You stay on the sidelines and cheer the staff on—appreciating all of their efforts, goodwill, and risk-taking. You don't punish the whole team for the faults of a few."

He continued, "My second belief is **If You Don't Feed the Teachers, They Eat the Students**. I go above and beyond to make sure the teachers who are doing their jobs—connecting with kids and fulfilling our mission—are rewarded, supported, and applauded." From that day forth, I have continually recognized outstanding administrators and noted their "Guy-isms." Thus, the birth of this book.

As Orlo L. Day, Guy's assistant principal for 16 years, stated, "Guy Bennett was among the best of those principals who could amalgamate teachers of widely varied personalities and backgrounds into what he liked to call 'a family,' each using God-given talents in making professional contributions to the intellectual and personal growth of students." Guy is missed deeply, but he left behind the legacy of a belief system that hopefully is addressed throughout the following pages.

Here's looking at you, Guy. ALOHA.

Table of Contents

Chapter 1

Whetting Your Appetite—
The Menu, Please!

Chapter 1

Whetting Your Appetite—
The Menu, Please!

◆ ◆ ◆

"The best teacher is the one who NEVER forgets
what it is like to be a student.
The best administrator is the one who NEVER forgets
what it is like to be a teacher."
–Neila A. Connors

◆ ◆ ◆

Let's begin with a reality—this book is not research-based, focused on results of surveys, or theoretically driven. The information is based on observations, discussions, personal learning experiences, shadowing, and "good ol' common sense." Like Frank Sinatra, "I did it MY WAY."

Consequently, if you are extremely left-brained and searching for statistics, micro-management strategies, or in-depth research studies to validate the forthcoming information, this book is NOT for you. On the other hand, if you are looking for some basic and practical ways to be an outstanding administrator, with "FUN" sprinkled throughout, read on. I hope you enjoy the "dining experience." Bon Appétit!

WHY DID I WRITE THIS BOOK?

Education is a serious business that requires every grain of "being" from individuals who want to invest in making a difference for students. It demands a serious commitment from people willing to go above and beyond the call of duty. Being an educator during these times is not easy. Why?

Plainly, educators are expected to deal with all of the issues and baggage children bring from their homes into learning settings. Children enter school doors every day either having just left a healthy, happy home where adults truly recognize the importance of a good education and raising self-directed children or having just left an empty house filled with empty promises and an empty refrigerator. On a daily basis, all walks of life arrive at school hoping they will be safe, fed, and assisted in realizing dreams. As Eleanor Roosevelt said, "The future belongs to those who believe in the beauty of their dreams."

Educators can make or break a child's day and ultimately impact their future. The power of a teacher is ongoing—whether it is positive or negative. Thus is the business of education. We must continually work together to recognize that we truly do touch the future—we teach. A difference is made when an individual teacher closes his/her door and connects with students. Consequently, to ensure that teachers are supportive of all students, we must create professional, safe, secure, and encouraging environments where everyone feels appreciated, listened to, and respected. Hence, the role of the administrator is the crucial element in determining the morale and climate of any given school.

So, why did I write this book? As someone, who spends an extraordinary amount of time in schools working with administrators and teachers, I saw a need for reflection. Through my personal experiences, I can irrefutably state that successful schools only survive when there are successful administrators leading the way. As simplistic as this may seem, effective schools exist and persevere only when an exceptional leader with a vision is the "head cook." Too often, the demise of a celebrated school occurs when a mediocre leader, who does not have the fire in her/his belly or passion to continue forging ahead, replaces a talented leader.

Successful administrators FEED their teachers continuously to make sure the students ARE NOT EATEN. Meaning, the best leaders focus on providing a climate where teachers are encouraged to take risks and act as coaches—guiding students through journeys of success. Effective leaders ask, guide, delegate, communicate, encourage, and take risks. They make it abundantly clear that the people in the building are important, and they'll do whatever it takes to say thank you for winning efforts.

I am continually impressed with outstanding teachers. Those teachers who have "overloaded plates," are minimally recognized or appreciated for their efforts. The student advocates who are sometimes forced to focus on a test-driven curriculum rather than a skills/process based curriculum are the real heroes. Consequently, I wanted to share some ways administrators can applaud and support these great teachers. I agree with my friend and mentor, Jim Garvin, who shares, "Teachers are the GOLD-COLLAR workers of the universe." If the information shared herein helps one administrator become a more positive, teacher-focused leader, I will be satisfied. In the meantime, here's a toast to all of those administrators who already effectively feed their teachers. You are the champions and the reason successful schools form the foundation of our society.

WHO NEEDS TO READ THIS BOOK?

Primarily, this book is for anyone who agrees that teaching is the most important profession there is. It needs to be read by individuals who recognize that teaching is difficult and teachers need continual appreciative acts. Whenever we can provide positive experiences to promote teachers and their efforts, we are on a winning track. This book is for all grade levels, all genders, all types of leaders, and all geographic locations. Most importantly, it is for anyone wanting to make a difference.

Secondly, it would help if the readers were well-adjusted leaders and in positions to implement the suggestions. Obviously, the more self-worth one has, the more likely she/he is to reflect, analyze, and determine how to improve. Who is well-adjusted?

The defining characteristics of a well-adjusted leader include:

• **THE ABILITY TO CARE AND BE CONCERNED FOR OTHERS**

Before anyone can make a difference they must care. The best schools are based on the premise that no one cares how much you know until they know how much you care. The leader of a school is instrumental in defining, developing, and designing a climate of care. From the moment you walk in the front door of a school, symbols of care must be prevalent throughout. It is the people, practices, positives, and performances that characterize the "caring-ness" of a school. An effective leader serves as the CARE police.

• **THE DESIRE TO BE SUCCESSFUL**

Success is defined as a "favorable outcome or result." Effective leaders are persistently in search of ways to improve, grow, and strengthen. Success begets success. Consequently, in surroundings where leaders are focused on pleasant results, outcomes are frequently rewarding to all. The best leaders walk the talk of success.

• **THE ABILITY TO HANDLE STRESS**

There is only one group of people who do not have stress in their lives and they are no longer on the planet. Stress is an element of life and it depends on how one handles this stress that makes or breaks a situation. Successful leaders respond to stress rather than react to it. They also include many stress–relievers in their communications. Chapter six will discuss handling stress in more detail.

• **A GENERAL FEELING OF GOOD HEALTH**

A healthy person is a happy person. Anyone who decides to take on a leadership position must realize the importance of good health. Our health is like sleep—we don't miss it until we are deprived of it. Valuable leaders recognize the importance of cherishing the mind, body, and spirit.

- **THE ABILITY TO THINK LOGICALLY**

  "Think before you speak" is one of the best pieces of advice a leader can internalize. The best leaders take the time to look at every decision with care, commitment, and connections—how will it affect others? Making time to reflect is crucial to successful leadership.

- **THE ABILITY TO HAVE FUN**

  Anyone who embarks upon a mission of leadership in education today MUST be able to have fun or they will ultimately be miserable. Education is a tough business that requires every possible bit of stamina and concentration. Therefore, the best leaders are those who have a great sense of humor and never let a day go by without laughing. In my opinion, a day without laughter is a day without living. The best schools are places where adults and students enjoy themselves and have fun.

  With this arsenal of defining characteristics, a well-adjusted leader is one who makes the difference. Hopefully, you are that person or you know one who can benefit from the proceeding pages. My goals are to applaud those already feeding the teachers, assist those who need to feed, and provide useful techniques to create a buffet of strategies to thank hard-working teachers.

WHERE DO YOU BEGIN? THE APPETIZER, PLEASE!

A truly successful leader is a reflective leader. Accordingly, I would encourage any leader to begin with a personal self-assessment to address individual areas of strength and need. The following ten questions are to be answered in order, and as quickly as possible. Mark your beginning time at the top of the questionnaire and your ending time at the conclusion. Do not move to the next question until you have answered the previous question.

◆ ◆ ◆

Starting Time _____

What is your most important professional goal?

_____

_____

Identify FIVE positive attributes about YOU.

1. _____
2. _____
3. _____
4. _____
5. _____

When is the next PLANNED time you will be spending with the important people in your life and what is the planned activity?

_____

_____

What is a professional RISK you have recently taken? (Include the date.)

_____

_____

What specific PERSONAL activity do you have PLANNED this week to do just for you ("me time")?

_____

How often do you REFLECT and in what way (thinking, journals, etc.)?

_____

What is something you have been avoiding? Commit to a time and date (in writing) when you will complete this activity.

_____

_____

On a scale of 1–10 (with 10 being the highest/perfect score) rate the following:

Your physical self? _____   Your professional self? _____

Your intellectual self? _____   Your emotional self? _____

Your social self? _____   Your spiritual self? _____

What is the overall average of your scores? _____

Write 3–5 goals you need to set to improve your average:

1. _____
2. _____
3. _____
4. _____
5. _____

Identify 10 strengths you have as a leader.

1. _____
2. _____
3. _____
4. _____
5. _____
6. _____
7. _____
8. _____
9. _____
10. _____

Complete the phrase, "I feel best about myself when _____

_____."

Ending Time _____

◆ ◆ ◆

As you look back over your responses, ask yourself these questions:

* What questions were the most difficult to answer?

_____

* How long did it take to answer the ten questions?

_____

* What areas need improvement and how will I do it?

_____

* From my responses, what is the basis of my personal mission statement?

_____

Future chapters will address each of the ten questions in length. It is important, however, that you take the time to self-assess so you can begin developing a personal mission statement. Great leaders have excellent interpersonal skills as well as being introspective. Many of the following chapters will involve deep thinking and introspection with the hopes that some of the tips and tactics will assist in your own personal development. May the adventure begin.

◆ ◆ ◆

" . . . to stick to one's guns come what may—
this is the gift of leadership."
–Mohandas K. Ghandi

◆ ◆ ◆

Chapter 2

The Need to Feed

◆ ◆ ◆

Chapter 2

The Need to Feed

◆ ◆ ◆

"Leadership—Making happen that in which you believe."
–Roland Barth

◆ ◆ ◆

A number of years ago, I was involved in a project identifying and shadowing outstanding teachers throughout the country. My main goal was to ascertain the common attributes of great teachers.

The most fulfilling aspect of the project was meeting and working with so many phenomenal educators. The most difficult part was narrowing the characteristics. The one commonality that was evident in every discussion, however, was the importance of leadership. When teachers were asked, "What is it that makes you so outstanding?" they readily remarked that they had an administrator who encouraged and supported them, trusted their professionalism, and made them feel like a significant member of a very important team. The testimony of these outstanding teachers re-emphasized the key role of administrative leadership.

If one hundred teachers were asked to define great leadership, we would probably get one hundred different definitions with common strands. However, in my opinion, the main characteristic of a great leader is someone whom others WANT to follow. A leader who creates a culture of nurturing and identifying talents (ultimately capitalizing on those unique talents) is one who "feeds" teachers on a continual basis.

Therefore, "Why feed the teachers?" should be an easy question to answer. Administrators who make it a priority to treat teachers with respect, recognize invaluable contributions, and realize teachers are their best allies, see great things happen. The returns are unlimited! Teachers are extraordinary resources that outstanding leaders acknowledge as vital components of successful schools.

Great leaders use teachers as resources for the following:

1. *TO SERVE AS SOLUTION FINDERS. The best thinkers spend 5% of their time discussing the problem and 95% of the time identifying solutions. When given the opportunity, teachers are excellent "outside of the box" thinkers. Many times, when given a challenge, the best leaders immediately convene with a group of teachers who will invariably identify a number of solutions. Sometimes impossible suggestions are presented, but they are invariably creative.*

2. *TO PROVIDE FEEDBACK. There is no way an administrator can single-handedly know everything that is occurring in the entire building. Consequently, an information system must be in place where teachers as resources can keep the administrators updated, informed, and knowledgeable so there are no surprises. When teachers are treated with trust, respect, and professionalism, they feel comfortable identifying flaws or informing the leadership that something may not be working effectively. They become the reality check for new practices, policies, and policing. They can also occasionally convince the leaders that some sacred cows make GREAT burgers!*

Administrators who strive for success through growing and improvement commonly ask teachers the following types of questions (either on a weekly update form or personally):

- *How was your week?*

- *What are some successes you experienced this week?*

- *Did you have any problems this week that the administrative team can assist you with?*

- *Are there any concerns you have about the overall operation of the school?*

- *Do you have any suggestions for improving our school?*

- *Do you have any suggestions for the administrative team to improve relationships and strive to achieve our mission?*

- *Do you have any needs (professional, janitorial, team, etc.) that are not presently being met, and how can we assist?*

When administrators take the time to ask for feedback and input, teachers feel as though their contributions make a difference. However, the best administrators never ask for information that they plan to ignore, and never ask for input on a decision they have already made. Teachers feel unimportant when they realize the request for input is not sincere or will not be regarded. Ongoing, positive, and student-focused advice becomes the essence of building a foundation for success in feeding teachers.

3. TO SPREAD THE GOOD WORD. In education we can be our own best friends or worst enemies. It depends on how we communicate to others in our community. The best leaders solicit the services of great teachers in meeting with community groups and organizations. Teachers as resources can be invaluable in explaining programs, new policies, or providing updates to parents and community members. When teachers are in a positive environment where they are treated professionally, they are more apt to share successes outside the school building.

One creative administrator, frustrated with the lack of participation on Parents Night, began a monthly "Our School is Great" program in a local grocery store. Once a month, a team of teachers would set up a booth in the store and share information about the school, provide calendars of upcoming events, and answer any questions from parents and community members. The results were extremely powerful in connecting with the townspeople.

Innovative administrators constantly work with teachers in finding ways to not only invite parents into the school community but also get the good word out to them. Through newsletters, web pages, e-mail, bulletin boards, community service projects, and a plethora of other means, educators who truly care about the school-home-community connection will go above and beyond to communicate the positives about the school and students.

4. TO SHARE THEIR TALENTS. Great leaders know that every "ORDINARY" person has a hidden "EXTRA" somewhere that makes them EXTRAORDINARY. There are so many unused talents in this country, and many of these unknown talents are in schools. Administrators, as talent scouts, must capitalize on every positive and provide a climate where the hidden talents are unveiled and people are encouraged to perform.

"What is the best way to discover talent?" Easy! Just ask people what is it they truly enjoy doing outside of their profession. Many times we are so busy with the business of school we forget to even realize that educators have a personal life. I am not suggesting that administrators must delve deeply into everyone's personal life outside of school. I am suggesting, however, that there must be opportunities for the people in schools to share interests, uniquenesses, and gifts with others. This can be accomplished through social gatherings, special interest clubs, faculty "what's up" boards, and other ways to make the people-connection important. Once great talents are exposed, great leaders find a way to spread the wealth and make people feel validated.

5. TO PROVIDE SUPPORT. Administration is a lonely business. I never realized how lonely until I left the classroom and became an administrator through an internship program. All of a sudden it was as if the administration was the enemy. This really rang true when dealing with discipline problems. Many times I would deal with a major problem of physical attack or threat, which was very difficult and emotional, and then be faced by a student who was sent to the office for going to class without a pencil. Yes, a student would be sent out of class to the office to sit and wait for an administrator to confront him/her on the reasons we NEVER go to class without a pencil. I am not an administrator, because my belief system would ask, "Couldn't the teacher handle this?" I would give the student a pencil and send them back to class. You know the rest of the story. I was the enemy because I did not remove body parts or force the student to repent for the rest of his or her life.

Consequently, an important message that I do not want to get short-changed or lost throughout this book is the fact that ADMINISTRATORS ALSO NEED TO BE FED. In successful schools where the adults recognize effective and caring leadership, they also return the goodwill. Random acts of kindness work both ways and teachers need to take the time to applaud, support, and recognize great leadership. Fulfilled teachers make it a priority to recognize the leadership by saying "we appreciate you" in as many ways as possible.

When exemplary administrators are asked what makes them so great they consistently respond, "the adults in this building." They see effectiveness as being synergistic and recognize that there is no "I" in LEADER. They also add that they could not be effective alone. Magnificent support systems are foundations for excellence and progress school-wide.

ARE YOUR TEACHERS HUNGRY?

Teachers are thirsty for great leadership. We all want to be appreciated and acknowledged. Walk through this scenario with me if you will. Think of a mentor—someone who has professionally inspired and influenced your life. Now picture a morning when you are preparing to go to school and the phone rings. Upon answering the phone, you are excited that it is your mentor who has taken the time to connect with you. This significant person begins to explain that the reason for the call is to tell you what a great person you are, how fortunate the world is to have you in it, and how you truly make a difference in the lives of others. They conclude with a few more accolades and wish you a happy day. What kind of day would you have? How would you feel? Would you feel invincible? We all know the answers. The lesson? Simply, genuinely building people up can affect their total outlook on life. Words of encouragement can affect everyone you touch throughout the day.

First, you need to determine the hunger pangs of your staff. The following simple self-assessment, which has been developed informally during the years through discussions, surveys, and observations, may provide some insight. It is based on common sense and information gathered from outstanding educators concerning how effective administrators lead. Answer each of the following questions by marking "yes" or "no" and then score yourself at the conclusion. Each question will be explained following the assessment.

___YES ___NO   1. Do you have a low teacher absentee rate?

___YES ___NO   2. Is it easy to ask teachers to do something not outlined in their contract?

___YES ___NO   3. Do teachers keep talking and include you in the conversation when you enter a room?

___YES ___NO   4. Do you easily get teachers to volunteer for additional activities?

___YES ___NO 5. Do you feel totally energized at the end of the day having accomplished many major tasks?

___YES ___NO 6. Do you readily walk into classrooms when teachers are teaching and/or doors are closed?

___YES ___NO 7. Do you spend the majority of your day out of your office and accessible?

___YES ___NO 8. Do teachers let you know how comfortable they are talking to you?

___YES ___NO 9. Do you discuss controversial issues with the faculty?

___YES ___NO 10. Do you look forward to and realistically schedule teacher evaluations?

___YES ___NO 11. Do you openly share your belief systems and expectations with all?

___YES ___NO 12. Do you encourage teachers to provide input and suggestions?

___YES ___NO 13. Do you regularly ask teachers to evaluate your effectiveness?

___YES ___NO 14. Do you schedule times to actually teach in a classroom and work with students?

___YES ___NO 15. Do you take an interest in your teachers' personal well-being?

___YES ___NO 16. Do you plan regular and ongoing socials for your staff?

___YES ___NO 17. Do you surprise teachers regularly with a note of thanks or a random act of kindness?

___YES ___NO 18. Do you avoid unwarranted distractions during the day (e.g., intercom announcements)?

___YES ___NO 19. Do you inform teachers of upcoming meetings in advance to allow time to plan for personal obligations?

___YES ___NO 20. Do your teachers proudly exhibit professionalism during meetings and in-service workshops (e.g., not working on other activities, not leaving at contracted time, etc.)?

___YES ___NO 21. Do you ask teachers to complete forms only once and then share results with the staff?

___YES ___NO 22. Do you have a monthly and weekly planning sheet that is shared with everyone?

___YES ___NO 23. Do you make it a practice to touch base with as many adults as possible every day?

___YES ___NO 24. Do you feel comfortable dropping by the teachers' lounge to chat?

___YES ___NO 25. Do you attempt to join different teachers at lunchtime to touch base?

___YES ___NO 26. Do you ask for input first and THEN make decisions based on the input?

___YES ___NO 27. Do you regularly hear teachers referring to you as supportive?

___YES ___NO 28. Do you believe you have a good understanding of the curriculum and activities in your school?

___YES ___NO 29. Do you enjoy making presentations and sharing promising practices at conferences to other educators?

___YES ___NO 30. Do you take every opportunity for your own personal and professional growth?

___YES ___NO 31. Do you encourage your staff to attend conferences, visit other schools, and learn from other resources?

___YES ___NO 32. Do you make it a priority to connect with parents and invite them into the school?

___YES ___NO 33. Do you make an effort to share effective practices and programs with community members and parents when in the community?

___YES ___NO 34. Do you make an effort to learn students' names and backgrounds?

___YES ___NO 35. Do students come to you to talk or ask for advice?

___YES ___NO 36. Do you feel knowledgeable about and included in all the student-oriented activities teachers are organizing for their students?

___YES ___NO 37. Do you feel comfortable discussing curriculum or discipline issues with parents?

___YES ___NO 38. Do you make an effort to arrange FUN activities for the staff and students?

___YES ___NO 39. Do you look forward to going to work every day?

___YES ___NO 40. Do you focus more on solutions than on problems?

___YES ___NO 41. Do you continually talk positively about your staff members to others?

___YES ___NO 42. Do you encourage student work to be displayed everywhere possible throughout the school?

___YES ___NO 43. Do you encourage students to be engaged in their climate and make suggestions to help?

___YES ___NO 44. Do you avoid silent lunches and school wide punishments?

___YES ___NO 45. Do you recognize that every teacher is different and allow them to conduct classrooms in a manner fitting to the needs of the students being taught ?

___YES ___NO 46. Do you admonish only the staff members in the wrong rather than implementing a new policy that punishes everyone?

___YES ___NO 47. Do you avoid embarrassing a staff member in front of peers, parents, and/or students?

___YES ___NO 48. Do you take the time to deal with teachers' needs and frustrations?

___YES ___NO 49. Do you ask for input on budget items, calendars, and meeting agendas?

___YES ___NO 50. Do you make your own personal/family time a top priority in your life?

◆ ◆ ◆

How did you do? Count up the number of "YES" answers and look at your score below.

41–50 marked YES — Your teachers are SATIATED. Great Job!

31–40 marked YES — Your teachers are SATISFIED. They need SNACKS!

21–30 marked YES — Your teachers are HUNGRY. They need nourishment immediately!

11–20 marked YES — Your teachers are FAMISHED. Send for MEALS ON WHEELS!

0–10 marked YES — Your teachers are EMACIATED. FIND A NEW PROFESSION!

When designing the assessment instrument, educators casually shared their top fifty indicators evident in successful schools. The results were organized accordingly and produced the instrument. As always, the list could be expanded, shortened, and/or consolidated. However, it provides a template to reflect, and the following pages explain the rationale behind each question.

According to the educators who were surveyed, the following indicators correlate with effective leadership:

INDICATOR 1. EFFECTIVE LEADERS HAVE A LOW TEACHER ABSENTEE RATE.

When people are satisfied in their work environment, they do not like to be absent. Great leaders create a climate where people want to be.

INDICATOR 2. EFFECTIVE LEADERS ENCOURAGE TEACHERS TO DO WHAT IS BEST FOR THEIR PROFESSION, SCHOOL, AND STUDENTS.

When leaders make teachers feel good about their profession, they are more willing to do whatever it takes to be successful. They are not driven by a contract but by their heart.

INDICATOR 3. EFFECTIVE LEADERS ARE INCLUDED IN CONVERSATIONS WITH TEACHERS.

Effective schools are places where everyone shares. A leader who includes teachers in conversations will be included in teachers' conversations. Trust must be developed through open, concise, and direct discussions.

INDICATOR 4. EFFECTIVE LEADERS INFLUENCE TEACHERS TO VOLUNTEER FOR ADDITIONAL ACTIVITIES.

Teachers who recognize the need to feed administrators also know how stressful administration can be. Therefore, they lend a hand to assist progress whenever they can. Finding people to volunteer is not difficult.

INDICATOR 5. EFFECTIVE LEADERS TAKE TIME TO PLAN, ORGANIZE, AND ACCOMPLISH "TO DO'S" WITHOUT BURNING OUT.

It is important to organize each day and determine the importance of tasks. Effective organization leads to effective implementation. Consequently, great leaders avoid procrastination and attempt to accomplish at least 1–5 tasks from their daily To Do List.

INDICATOR 6. EFFECTIVE LEADERS VISIT CLASSROOMS.

Teachers continually share that effective leaders take the time to visit as many classrooms as possible. The best teachers truly enjoy the administrators coming into their classroom and observing daily activities. A closed door would never prevent a caring leader from entering a lab of learning.

INDICATOR 7. EFFECTIVE LEADERS ARE VISIBLE AND ACCESSIBLE.

The best leaders are seen throughout the building. They are accessible— spending as little time as possible in their office with a closed door. They have a management style of cruising classrooms and hallways.

INDICATOR 8. EFFECTIVE LEADERS ENJOY COMMUNICATING WITH TEACHERS.

When an environment is created where conversations are invited through questions and pondering, people share. Leaders who want to keep their fingers on the pulse of the school set up as many opportunities to talk personally with the staff as possible.

INDICATOR 9. EFFECTIVE LEADERS DISCUSS CONTROVERSIAL ISSUES WITH FACULTY MEMBERS.

Good debates and discussions clarify issues. An administrator who is self-assured and confident will want to hear the opinions of faculty members on new initiatives, trends, and mandates. A FED faculty can deal with controversy in a mature and professional manner.

INDICATOR 10. EFFECTIVE LEADERS SEE TEACHER EVALUATIONS AS EXTREMELY IMPORTANT.

The best leaders recognize the need for evaluations and make a plan to schedule them throughout the year avoiding the last minute syndrome. They also, however, realize that evaluations need to be a positive and growing experience with time for reflection and self-assessment.

INDICATOR 11. EFFECTIVE LEADERS SHARE THEIR BELIEFS AND EXPECTATIONS WITH ALL.

Teachers continually remark how refreshing it is to work with an individual who shares, cares, and dares. People want to know what the leader believes and what he/she expects. The best leaders don't have hidden agendas and readily communicate to all involved.

INDICATOR 12. EFFECTIVE LEADERS CONTINUOUSLY ASK FOR INPUT FROM STAFF MEMBERS.

Leaders know that to be effective, you must involve others. As discussed earlier, teachers are the best resources an administrator has. When others are asked for their ideas, philosophies, and thinking, it makes one reprocess his or her own beliefs. Input from all is essential in building a staff.

INDICATOR 13. EFFECTIVE LEADERS ASK STAFF MEMBERS TO EVALUATE THEM.

The most secure leaders want to provide opportunities for staff members to evaluate their effectiveness. Regular "How am I Doing?" sessions or forms are imperative.

INDICATOR 14. EFFECTIVE LEADERS SCHEDULE TIMES TO WORK WITH STUDENTS.

The best leaders will say that the finest stress reliever is to get away from the office and plan an activity with students. Teachers admire administrators that take time to personally interact with students. Students love it, too!

INDICATOR 15. EFFECTIVE LEADERS TAKE A PERSONAL INTEREST IN THE WELL-BEING OF PEOPLE ON THE STAFF.

Wellness is essential for anyone to work in the field of education today. Leaders who care about the whole person take time to ask about personal life, provide discussions for wellness, and monitor morale continually.

INDICATOR 16. EFFECTIVE LEADERS PLAN REGULAR SOCIAL ACTIVITIES FOR THE STAFF.

As the title of the book indicates, feeding (literally and figuratively) is important. Teachers need opportunities to get together and just enjoy each other's company. Many times an impromptu social is more valuable than one that was extensively planned.

INDICATOR 17. EFFECTIVE LEADERS TAKE THE TIME TO SHOW APPRECIATION.

A quick note of thanks, a small coupon for a burger, or even an apple to say, "You're great" can make such a difference in a teacher's day. Everyone blossoms through appreciative acts.

INDICATOR 18. EFFECTIVE LEADERS AVOID UNNECESSARY DISTRACTIONS THROUGHOUT THE DAY.

The best leader is the one who never forgets what it is like to be a teacher. Consequently, effective leaders do everything in their power not to disrupt the flow of the school day unless absolutely necessary. The intercom is used only as a last resort.

INDICATOR 19. EFFECTIVE LEADERS INFORM ALL OF UPCOMING MEETINGS AND AGENDAS.

The best leaders realize that teachers have a life, family, and responsibilities outside of education. Therefore, in scheduling meetings, the best leaders give everyone involved enough advance notice to make the necessary arrangements. An agenda is also imperative so professionals will come prepared. Most importantly, meetings are relevant, timely, and productive.

INDICATOR 20. EFFECTIVE LEADERS ARE TREATED WITH RESPECT DURING MEETINGS AND WORKSHOPS.

An environment that models respect creates respect. Teachers who admire the leadership make sure all of their actions demonstrate a mature and professional attitude. They listen, participate, and don't engage in other activities during meetings or other professional engagements.

INDICATOR 21. EFFECTIVE LEADERS ASK TEACHERS FOR INFORMATION ONLY ONCE.

Teaching requires endless paperwork. Thus, teachers complain when asked to complete forms asking the same information more than once. The best leaders are sensitive to the amount of information they request from teachers and the amount of time given to obtain the data.

INDICATOR 22. EFFECTIVE LEADERS DISTRIBUTE MONTHLY AND WEEKLY PLANNING SHEETS TO KEEP EVERYONE UPDATED.

So many things happen in a given day, week, and month that is it very difficult to be informed unless someone organizes all activities. Administrators know the importance of keeping everyone up to date.

INDICATOR 23. EFFECTIVE LEADERS CONNECT WITH AS MANY ADULTS AS POSSIBLE EACH DAY.

Leaders who truly care about the people in the building take the time to let them know. A simple "Good morning!" or "How are you doing?" can make a big difference and start someone's day off on a positive note.

INDICATOR 24. EFFECTIVE LEADERS CONNECT WITH TEACHERS ON BREAK.

The best leaders feel comfortable dropping in on the teachers during break whether it is in the lounge or elsewhere. There is no "off limits" in a school where everyone feels welcomed and important.

INDICATOR 25. EFFECTIVE LEADERS DINE WITH TEACHERS WHEN POSSIBLE.

Some of the best conversations held are during a dining experience. When an administrator takes the time to eat and chat with teachers, they make the teachers feel special.

INDICATOR 26. EFFECTIVE LEADERS BASE DECISIONS ON THE INPUT REQUESTED.

One of the biggest frustrations to people is being asked for input when the final decisions have already been made. It is an insult to professionalism. Thus, true leaders ensure that when input is solicited it will be considered.

INDICATOR 27.   EFFECTIVE LEADERS ARE SUPPORTIVE.

Teachers need support and the best leaders recognize this need. The best leaders do whatever it takes to provide the resources for the staff.

INDICATOR 28.   EFFECTIVE LEADERS CAN EFFECTIVELY ARTICULATE CURRICULAR ACTIVITIES OCCURRING SCHOOL-WIDE.

The difference between a good leader and a great leader is that a good leader can explain what is happening throughout the school with little hesitation. A GREAT leader not only explains ongoing activities but also does so with a passion and enthusiasm that is flattering and contagious.

INDICATOR 29.   EFFECTIVE LEADERS PRESENT USEFUL INFORMATION AND PRACTICES TO OTHERS.

Great leaders have so much to share that others can learn from. The best administrators are commonly found presenting to community organizations, other administrators, school boards, and conferences. Great administrators are also great teachers.

INDICATOR 30.   EFFECTIVE LEADERS RECOGNIZE THE IMPORTANCE OF ONGOING PERSONAL AND PROFESSIONAL GROWTH.

You don't know what you don't know, so the best administrators strive to learn, grow, and improve both personally and professionally. They take every afforded chance to increase their skills and knowledge.

INDICATOR 31.   EFFECTIVE LEADERS RECOGNIZE THE IMPORTANCE OF TEACHERS ATTENDING CONFERENCES AND WORKSHOPS.

Authentic leaders believe that teachers need to attend conferences, workshops, and be involved in any experience which benefits students. Teachers need opportunities to rejuvenate, revalidate, and recommit to their profession.

INDICATOR 32. EFFECTIVE LEADERS CONNECT WITH PARENTS.

The best leaders know that the partnership with parents is imperative in the success of a school. They make an ongoing commitment to involve, inform, and indulge parents.

INDICATOR 33. EFFECTIVE LEADERS CONNECT WITH THE COMMUNITY.

Successful schools have a strong community backing. This backing comes from the efforts of a strong administrator to inform and involve the community through service projects, positive media, and any other means of including the parents and community.

INDICATOR 34. EFFECTIVE LEADERS LEARN STUDENTS' NAMES AND BACKGROUNDS.

In student-oriented schools, you see administrators conversing, caring, and connecting with students throughout the day. The affective component is a major characteristic of a school for students.

INDICATOR 35. EFFECTIVE LEADERS ARE AVAILABLE TO STUDENTS.

When students are asked to describe great administrators, they say the ones who "are nice and talk to you." Students need as many stable adults in their lives as possible. A great leader can provide this strength.

INDICATOR 36. EFFECTIVE LEADERS ARE AWARE OF THE ONGOING STUDENT ACTIVITIES AVAILABLE.

Great schools have a curriculum that is ongoing in the hallways, lunchrooms, and other places outside of classrooms. The best leaders can articulate and participate in the many different ways teachers connect positively with students.

INDICATOR 37. EFFECTIVE LEADERS ARE INVOLVED IN DISCUSSING CURRICULUM AND DISCIPLINE WITH PARENTS.

A terrific administrator feels comfortable being involved in curriculum and discipline discussions between parents and teachers. They are recognized as leaders of instruction and behavior in the school.

INDICATOR 38. EFFECTIVE LEADERS MAKE "FUN" AN IMPORTANT COMPONENT OF EVERY DAY.

The best leaders know that people having fun are more likely to be creative, take risks, and enjoy their job. Upon entering a building for the first time, one can instantly recognize the "fun factor" being applied.

INDICATOR 39. EFFECTIVE LEADERS LOOK FORWARD TO GOING TO WORK.

What more can you say? If you are happy in your job and fulfilled, you will be happy in your life. Life is too short to spend it in a miserable work situation.

INDICATOR 40. EFFECTIVE LEADERS ARE SOLUTION FINDERS.

It is easy to sit around and "quack" about the problems of a profession. It is hard to find solutions. However, the best leaders focus on doable, people-oriented solutions.

INDICATOR 41. EFFECTIVE LEADERS ARE PROUD TO TELL OTHER PEOPLE ABOUT THE GREAT THINGS THEIR STAFF DOES.

Leaders who acknowledge and applaud their staff outwardly are rewarded inwardly. The best administrators are constantly singing the praises of others.

INDICATOR 42. EFFECTIVE LEADERS ENCOURAGE STUDENT WORK TO BE DISPLAYED IN AS MANY PLACES AS POSSIBLE.

People are more important than paint and the best administrators want the students to own the walls. Students enjoy seeing their work displayed and great leaders want others to take pride in everyone's success.

INDICATOR 43.   EFFECTIVE LEADERS INVOLVE STUDENTS IN DECISION MAKING.

Schools were built for students and the best administrators never forget this. They take the time to talk to students about what is working, what is not, and how the school can be improved.

INDICATOR 44.   EFFECTIVE LEADERS DISCOURAGE SCHOOL-WIDE PUNISHMENTS.

Everyone makes mistakes, and yes, decisions to deal with problems must be made. The best leaders, however, never punish the entire school for the faults of a few. They deal with the specific problems and individuals as they occur.

INDICATOR 45.   EFFECTIVE LEADERS APPRECIATE AND APPLAUD TEACHERS' INDIVIDUAL METHODS AND PRACTICES.

The best leaders do not confine teachers with rules and regulations that make them teach one certain way. They appreciate and respect that the best teachers do what they have to do to ensure success for all.

INDICATOR 46.   EFFECTIVE LEADERS DEAL EFFECTIVELY AND EFFICIENTLY WITH INEFFECTIVE TEACHERS.

The best leaders admonish only the staff members in the wrong rather than implementing a new policy that punishes everyone. They are fair and do not tolerate incompetence or status quo.

INDICATOR 47.   EFFECTIVE LEADERS NEVER EMBARRASS OR PUT DOWN A STAFF MEMBER IN FRONT OF OTHERS.

The best leaders deal with conflicts directly and individually. They never treat anyone with disrespect or disregard for their feelings.

INDICATOR 48. *EFFECTIVE LEADERS DEAL IMMEDIATELY AND INDIVIDUALLY WITH TEACHERS' NEEDS AND FRUSTRATIONS.*

Caring leaders take the time to help teachers. They recognize the importance of creating a worthy environment for all.

INDICATOR 49. *EFFECTIVE LEADERS INVOLVE THE STAFF INSOFAR AS POSSIBLE IN BUDGET, CALENDAR, AND AGENDA ITEMS.*

Input, input, input. It is essential in running effective schools. Teachers continuously have opportunities to have a say about the budget, scheduled activities, and meetings (format, agenda, etc.).

INDICATOR 50. *EFFECTIVE LEADERS HAVE A LIFE OUTSIDE OF EDUCATION.*

The best leaders know that they have to plan time for themselves and their families before their profession. The most stressed-out leaders are ones who consistently put their personal life last.

In conclusion, administrators must first recognize the strengths of their staff. They must realize that together they can make a difference, although it takes considerable reflection, commitment, and work. Leading into the 21st century will be both exciting and difficult. There will be many more opportunities for educators to develop themselves to their full potential, yet there will also be many more challenges. To face these challenges, leaders must collaborate, communicate, and celebrate. The table is set.

◆ ◆ ◆

"IT TAKES ALL OF US . . .
For the woods would be very silent
if no birds sang except the best."
–Henry Van Dyke

◆ ◆ ◆

Chapter 3

Creating the Ambiance—
Preparing to Dine

◆ ◆ ◆

Chapter 3

Creating the Ambiance—
Preparing to Dine

◆ ◆ ◆

"The quality of employees will be directly proportional
to the quality of life you maintain for them."
–Charles E. Bryan

◆ ◆ ◆

*Envision the following scenario: Your friends have invited you for dinner and
have made all of the arrangements to dine at a new establishment in town.
You arrive at the restaurant fifteen minutes before your reservation and notice
everyone standing outside. Someone from the restaurant is barking
directions at the customers, explaining that they may not enter for another
fifteen minutes. It is rather chilly outside, but you do as you are told. At the
designated time, an unhappy hostess opens the door and shouts further
directions. Everyone immediately rushes into the building, frantically pushing
and shoving. Upon entering, you immediately notice the stark, drab
atmosphere with "Do Not . . ." signs displayed everywhere telling people
what they cannot do. The walls are a grayish white-yellow, and the paint is
peeling. The windows are clad with ragged, dirty shades. The facility is in
need of a thorough and detailed cleaning.*

*A waiter comes to the table to review the list of unacceptable behaviors and
explains that you have only forty-seven minutes in which to consume your pre-
selected dinner, as other diners are waiting for your table. You may not use the
restrooms during the time you spend at the table. Immediately your food is
delivered—some of it recognizable, some not. As you dine, trying to enjoy the
experience, your waiter continues to inform you of the remaining time at the
table. As your time nears the end, other diners begin to hover over your table,
anxious for their seats. At once, you are given the bill and told it is time to
depart from the table.*

Definitely not an encounter one wants to repeat. Why? Obviously neither the ambiance nor the climate is conducive to a fine dining experience, and the people are far from friendly. Do any of these experiences remind you of your school?

Twenty-first century administrators must recognize the importance of monitoring climate. Climate is defined as "the prevailing circumstances or set of attitudes influencing environmental conditions characterizing a group." A positive climate is what sets the tone for success in schools, and the best leaders work diligently to establish and maintain a place where people want to be. These leaders continually monitor, assess, and/or enhance the following major elements of a positive school climate:

1. *SAFETY. Schools must provide a safe place for all the inhabitants to be without any fear of being harmed. Parents collectively agree that the number one factor of importance to them is a safe environment for their children. A secure school is not only clean and healthy but also provides a setting for physical, intellectual, emotional, and social safety.*

   • *Physical Safety—Obviously, in a time of concern for all, schools must be places where students and adults do not feel afraid. Administrators must work to communicate the need for the adults in the building to scrutinize prevalent attitudes, activities, and ongoing actions in the school. Everyone must work together in keeping their fingers on the pulse of the school in order to recognize potential dangers and conflicts. In addition, effective leaders have a CRISIS PLAN in existence that everyone is aware of in case of a potential problem. This crisis plan must be thoroughly communicated and understood by all. The one commonality shared by all of the community members who recently experienced devastating evils in their schools was the statement, "We never thought it would happen here." The best leaders know that PREVENTION produces better results than INTERVENTION.*

   • *Intellectual Safety—Students and adults need to be respected for who they are and the gifts they possess. In intellectually safe schools, everyone feels significant. Programs and practices are in place that never humiliate, harm, or belittle another person. Ongoing opportunities exist to teach that failure is not fatal.*

- *Emotional Safety—The most effective school provides a climate where everyone feels as though they belong and the emphasis is on positive relationships. An ethos of caring prevails where adults take time with students and model stability. Programs are in place that give students opportunities for free discussions of their dreams, concerns, challenges, and needs. Adults take the time to talk and listen to students.*

- *Social Safety—School is a place for student socialization. Effective leaders take the time to provide positive socializing experiences for both the students and teachers. The walls are covered with student work and it is a place where everybody is somebody. Leaders who focus on social safety take the time to teach appropriate social behaviors to those lacking the knowledge.*

2. *CHANGE. We hear over and over that change is a process, not an event, and the best administrators recognize that to grow and improve one must change. Change, however, is not easy. The saying goes that a wet baby is the only one who enjoys change, yet with our society changing so rapidly, schools must be proactive. Leaders need to recognize that to have effective change, people must change; and for people to change, their realities and/or perceptions must change. In providing a climate of change, leaders become change agents. They must encourage innovation, collaboration, and creativity. In addition, they must applaud risk taking while realizing only "people-based" change will be effective in the long term. Openness to change enriches personal and professional lives.*

Effective leaders have a support structure that allows them to tune in to changes to meet student needs and make the school better. They also believe in grilling the "sacred cows" that are not working, which in turn challenges the system. These leaders recognize the uniquenesses of people who are effective in planning, producing, and implementing change.

Characteristics of effective leaders include:

- *A sense of self-worth, a positive attitude, and a belief in success.*

- *A purpose in life.*

- A love for life and the ability to face each day with zest, enthusiasm, and their best foot forward.

  •A willingness to always look at a better way to accomplish something.

  •A team player mentality.

  •A personal mission that includes continual rejuvenation and revitalization.

  •An open mind and eagerness to listen to others' opinions and options.

  •An excitement for new initiatives.

  •A sense of humor and ability to laugh at themselves.

Caring leaders also realize that educators' plates are already filled and running over. Therefore, they are sensitive to this issue and do not try to generate too much change at one time.

The best administrators address the issue of change using the following steps:

STEP ONE:
Invite discussion to address programs and/or practices that need change.

STEP TWO:
Identify a team of change agents to research the present status and the possible outcomes as a result of change.

STEP THREE:
Establish a vision and a strategy through the change team and communicate it to all who request input.

STEP FOUR:
Attempt to do away with any impediments to the change.

STEP FIVE:
Encourage risk-taking and recognize gains.

STEP SIX:
Implement the plan and monitor benchmarks of growth throughout the process.

STEP SEVEN:
Continually assess and report the status of effectiveness.

STEP EIGHT:
Readjust, monitor, revise, and start over if necessary.

STEP NINE:
Communicate, communicate, communicate!

STEP TEN:
Celebrate and reward success.

The truth is that through any change 5% of the people will accept it immediately, 25% will slowly adapt and accept, 60% will take a "let's wait and see" approach and will eventually accept the new idea if it works to their advantage, and 10% will never accept any change. The most astute leaders recognize this and DON'T WASTE TIME FERTILIZING ROCKS OR WATERING WEEDS. They work with the critical mass and reward those who forge ahead. The Japanese term for continual improvement is kaizen. It is a never-ending pursuit to improve and advance. Effective leaders promote this philosophy.

Additionally, leaders as change agents search out the best resources available. One of the best resources for leaders involved in change is the book <u>Who Moved My Cheese</u> by Spencer Johnson, M.D. This book uses a metaphorical approach to provide great lessons in the process of change.

◆ ◆ ◆

"If you always do what you've always done,
you'll always get what you've always got."
–Ed Foreman

◆ ◆ ◆

3. *POSITIVE ATTITUDES. Every day we rise, put on our clothes, and put on our attitude. I truly believe that a positive attitude and outlook on life is the foundation for triumph. EVERYTHING revolves around one's attitude and the outstanding leaders of our schools model this consistently. Someone once said, "You can have a positive attitude without talent and you can have talent without a positive attitude, but things really start happening when you have a positive attitude combined with talent." The best leaders exhibit the combination of the two.*

Unfortunately, there are some people who suffer from psycho-sclerosis, which is a hardening of the attitude. They blame their negative attitude on the negativism in newspapers, the media, and our society. Or, they blame the politicians, the heroes that mess up, or their relationships. Some even blame other people or their job description. The problem is, they are so busy blaming that they fail to take a deep look at their inner being. They fail to recognize that they are in control of their own attitude and no one else can determine their thoughts.

When teachers are asked what makes it difficult to maintain a positive attitude, you hear many of the same reasons worldwide. These include: non-supportive parents, over-indulgent parents, disruptive and empathetic students, an overload of paperwork and mandates, a hurried curriculum, a society driven by test results, poor physical conditions, low pay, lack of resources, limited technology, large class sizes, negative colleagues, under-funded incentive plans, a critical society, a concern for safety, and unsupportive administrators. Hopefully, there is not one school that deals with all of the above issues but every school could probably identify at least one area that is in critical need. In addition to many forces working against us, we also must deal with the CLIMATE CONTROLLERS within the school.

The four types of Climate Controllers are as follows:

1. *THE CLIMATE BUSTERS. This group works very hard on bursting balloons of enthusiasm and effort. They are commonly heard saying, "It can't be done, that won't work, we tried that in 1953—it didn't work then and won't work now." They find glory in shooting down any new ideas and initiatives by energized and student-focused adults.*

2. *THE CLIMATE MANIPULATORS. This group attempts to keep the rumor mill in business and spend a great deal of time putting one group or person against another. They are often found asking, "Did you hear about, or do you know the REAL reason why . . . " They enjoy seeing others at odds and rarely communicate openly and honestly.*

3. *THE CLIMATE CRUISERS. This group is harmless. They basically cruise to work every day and go through the same routine—usually parking in the same spot and carrying the same bag for years. They are known for laminating their lesson plans and repeating the same lesson over and over for days, weeks, months, and years. Many ask, "How can they be that way and not burn out?" Simple—you can't burn out if you've NEVER been on FIRE. Members of this group are extremely deficient in the enthusiasm department.*

4. *THE CLIMATE IMPROVERS. This is the group that we worry about the most. The best leaders recognize them as the movers and shakers but the most apt for BURNOUT. They are always in that top 30% of change initiators and go above and beyond the call of duty. They have a pride for their school and a respect for their profession. Most importantly, they like the students they teach and support the administration openly.*

Climate improvers, which of course include great leaders, also demonstrate and express the following beliefs because one person with a true belief is worth more than ninety-nine with an interest.

- *A BELIEF IN YOURSELF. To be successful, one must have the confidence necessary to realize how important he or she is. This means recognizing that "ulcers are the result of climbing molehills" and days should not be spent with "can'ts." Begin each day with the question, "What wonderful things will I engage in today?"*

- *A BELIEF IN YOUR POTENTIAL. In a world with so many challenges, educators must realize the difference they make in the lives of so many students. As Eleanor Roosevelt said, "No one can make you feel inferior without your consent." Many lives are saved and successes made due to the influence of great teachers.*

- *A BELIEF IN YOUR PROFESSION. Educators are in the most important profession in the world. There is no career more difficult. Most people who criticize educators and schools could not perform the required tasks in a school for one day, let alone an entire year. Therefore, as professionals, we must believe in what we do and profess our pride throughout the community. My biggest frustration related to education is seeing people in the business who really do not like teaching and do not like students. We should have zero tolerance for uncaring and uninvolved educators. The most important question we must ask ourselves daily is, "If we had it to do all over again, would we choose the same profession?" When our answer is a resounding "YES," we are climate improvers.*

- *A BELIEF IN PEOPLE. In general, people are basically good. Positive people believe in others and look for the gold in everyone. As educators, we MUST believe that every student enters our school with wrapped gifts that we must help them unwrap, and beautiful dreams that we must help them turn into goals.*

◆ ◆ ◆

"A healthy person goes "Yes," "No," and "Whoopee!"
and an unhealthy person goes "Yes, but," "No, but," and "No Whoopee."
–Eric Berne

◆ ◆ ◆

4. OPEN COMMUNICATION. Most of the problems and concerns in today's schools are direct results of the failure to communicate. Effective leaders realize that there is no way one can OVER-communicate. Consequently, open communication is ongoing and involves everyone. As Carla O'Dell stated, "If you don't give people information, they'll make up something to fill the void."

Many times when communication is discussed only one or two facets are recognized. The top administrators understand that communication includes listening and speaking along with reading, writing, thinking and feedback. A true communicator is one who employs all these tools effectively, is a model to others, and takes pride in his or her skills.

Suggestions for becoming a true communicator include:

- LISTENING—Mark Twain once said, "If we were to speak more than we were to listen, God would have given us two mouths instead." True listening is an art and administrators who are ranked among the best are always identified as having a talent for listening. The EAR model is a practical means for successful listening:
  - **E: Explore. Use open-ended questions and observe non-verbal messages.**
  - **A: Acknowledge by paraphrasing what you believe was said.**
  - **R: Respond using the least amount of time.**

- SPEAKING—George Bernard Shaw said, "The greatest problem with communication is the illusion that it has been accomplished." How true. Effective leaders take pride in speaking eloquently, concisely, and honestly. They use every means available to inform the educators, students, and parents of valuable information. They take pride in speaking to others and practice their communication skills to avoid the many distracters commonly used by adults and students such as "like," "and," "um," "er," and "uh." They speak with confidence and encourage other educators to do the same.

- READING—Being a realist, I know how difficult it is to do all that is expected of administrators in the 21st century. Yet, it is important that they keep current on trends, practices, and research. True leaders are readers and force some time each week into their schedule to scan recent journals, articles, and other media. Some schools have even started book clubs. Interested adults meet once a month at someone's house or a restaurant to discuss a current reading. Other leaders have implemented Sustained Silent Reading (SSR) programs where

EVERYONE in the school reads every day for 10–15 minutes. This provides educators with a scheduled time to indulge in a self-rewarding practice, while setting a living example for their students. If your "to be read" file sitting on the floor is taller than you are, some adjustments in your schedule are in order.

- WRITING—Effective leaders take pride in everything they write and share. They also take steps to ensure that any document written by anyone in the school models effective writing. There are more ways to communicate effectively through writing than ever before. Good administrators work to ensure that everyone receives weekly written updates and/or weekly e-mails (if appropriate), and has access to a school-wide bulletin board that also posts important information. The goal is to never hear any adult in the building say, "I didn't know about that meeting. I never received the information."

- THINKING—Administrative leaders depend on the fine resources within their building. They organize "think teams" to help them in developing mission statements, defining vision, solving problems, and becoming progressive. No leader, no matter how great he or she is, can do it alone. Leaders must also spend time reflecting on their own personal mission and vision.

- FEEDBACK—An integral ingredient of communication that is sometimes neglected is meaningful and concise feedback. EVERYONE wants to know how they are doing, if they could be doing better, and if there are suggestions for improvement. The best administrators continually feed the teachers through positive and/or constructive feedback delivered in a caring and compassionate manner.

5. HUMAN RELATIONS SKILLS. Treat a person as he is, and he will become what he is. Treat a person as he could be, and he will become what he can be. This is a vital concept for leaders to understand as they attempt to create an effective school climate. Positive and caring relationships are the heart of what makes a school extraordinary. The best leaders work on building an environment of respect, trust, professionalism, caring, compassion, collaboration, teaming, advising, encouraging, and nurturing. They share and practice the following:

The six most important words: . . . . . I admit I made a mistake.

The five most important words: . . . . . You did a great job.

The four most important words: . . . . What is YOUR opinion?

The three most important words: . . . . If you please . . .

The two most important words: . . . . . Thank you.

The one most important word: . . . . . WE

The least important word: I

6. ACTIVE PARTICIPATION BY ALL. For a school climate to truly meet the needs of all, all parties must be team players. The best leaders realize that when they create an atmosphere where people are truly participants rather than spectators, the leader does not have total control. The focus is on what needs to be done, how to do it, and what outcomes will be celebrated. The more people feel involved, the more they will volunteer, support the mission, and spread the good word. More participation means fewer cliques and control mechanisms.

7. POSITIVE PUBLIC RELATIONS. Last, but certainly not least, the positive climate must include a plan for positive communication with parents and the community. Good schools are everyone's business. Astute administrators know that the more they share promising practices, gains, successes, and celebrations with the public, the more support they will gain. The best schools are based on a family model where parents and community members feel welcomed and supported by the educators and feel no hesitation in visiting the school or asking questions of the administration.

Recognizing the importance and significance of climate, we must all realize that one does not have to be sick to get better and the room for improvement is always big enough for all of us. Yes, as a fine restaurant, a fine school gives the best service from the beginning of the day to the end and from one month to the next until the year ends. The leaders who make the difference also have a philosophy that it is their day and no one is going to ruin it.

The following strategies contribute to a healthy and happy climate:

1. PLAN "ME-TIME" AND "WE-TIME." *Your profession CANNOT be your sole priority. You need time for YOU (me-time) and for the significant others in your life (we-time). Most unhappy people do not have healthy relationships, a personal support group, or a life outside of work.*

2. VIEW PROBLEMS AS CHALLENGES. *Outstanding leaders spend 5% of their time discussing problems and 95% looking for solutions. They enforce this philosophy in every aspect of their life.*

3. DON'T BE A FINGER-POINTER. *Blame has never accomplished anything. Instead of spending time trying to figure out who is at fault, use the time to make things better.*

4. ANALYZE YOUR STRESSES AND FRUSTRATIONS. *Know what jerks your chain and avoid it. Don't set yourself up for additional health problems by overloading, procrastinating, or visiting with certain people who you will allow to irritate you.*

5. SET PERSONAL AND PROFESSIONAL GOALS. *Goals are dreams with deadlines and all effective leaders have a vision, a path, and a mission. It is best to ride the horse in the direction it is moving and have a plan mapped out for your final destination.*

6. DO NOT VEGETATE, PROCRASTINATE, OR NEGATIVATE. *Be active, organized, and positive. Get involved and be a part of the accomplishment.* HEALTHY PEOPLE ARE DOERS.

7. HAVE POSITIVE ROLE MODELS AND MENTORS. *Learn from others. A day without learning is a day not fully lived. There are lessons around us every day. Take advantage of any opportunity to talk to a mentor.*

8. *DON'T SPEND YOUR TIME TRYING TO PIN JELL-O TO WALLS. People who get bent out of shape by the little stuff never really grow much. When challenges occur, ask yourself if this will make any difference tomorrow, next week, or next month. Take your job seriously; take yourself lightly.*

9. *POSTURE YOURSELF AS A PROUD AND CONFIDENT PROFESSIONAL. Even on the days you don't feel your best, FAKE IT TILL YOU MAKE IT. A walk of confidence and pride definitely adds to the positive climate of a building.*

10. *DON'T EVER STOP PLAYING AND LAUGHING. A day without laughter is also a day not fully lived. There is so much to smile about in our business; and we know that we don't stop playing because we grow old—we grow old because we stop playing.*

The bottom line is that every one of us contributes to the ambiance or climate in the building. How we live every day, our every action, and our every word is our CHOICE.

Great leaders bring out the best in people and help them in choosing an attitude worth sharing. Your attitude is not determined by circumstances, but by how you RESPOND to those circumstances.

◆ ◆ ◆

"If you're working in a company that is NOT enthusiastic,
energetic, creative, clever, curious, and just plain fun,
you've got troubles, serious troubles."
                                        –Tom Peters

◆ ◆ ◆

Chapter 4

The Administrator as Master Chef—
Pass the P's, Please!

Chapter 4

The Administrator as Master Chef—
Pass the P's, Please!

◆ ◆ ◆

"Great administrators are like great chefs.
They both spend an inordinate amount of time preparing, planning,
and visioning before they even begin to COOK or implement.
During this time, they keep their focus on the outcomes and the clients.
They continuously re-adjust, refocus, and re-evaluate their plans and efforts."
–N. A. Connors

◆ ◆ ◆

As discussed previously, being an administrator in the 21st century is not easy. It takes very special people with very special gifts. Experienced educators value leaders who respect and recognize effort, provide opportunities to make a difference, walk the talk of fairness, allow open and engaged discussions, and provide an honest and flexible work environment. Consequently, when observing, interviewing, and learning from the best, I have concluded that the best CHEFS (Chief Heads Envisioning Future Successes) of a school exhibit the following P's:

THEY HAVE:

- *Positive attitudes*

- *Pleasing personalities*

- *Passion for their profession*

- *Purpose*

- *Patience*

- *Persistence*

THEY ARE:

- *People-oriented*

- *Prepared*

- *Present*

- *Prompt*

- *Praising*

- *Problem solvers*

- *Procrasti-blasters*

- *Pressure players*

- *Performance-based*

- *Proactive and Productive*

- *Parent- and public-minded*

Although some of these attributes have already been minimally addressed, they will be discussed in more detail, because repetition is the best teacher. Additionally, the following is like a menu. Please, select dishes that fit your needs.

POSITIVE ATTITUDES

If you have ever worked in or had the opportunity to closely observe the infrastructure of a first rate restaurant, you know that there is a major player who influences the mood of the evening. It is the chef. There is something about the chef that can make or break the evening, and we all know what that is. Give up? It is the same factor that determines your existence, your every day, and your success in life. As discussed in previous chapters, ATTITUDE IS THE ESSENCE OF LIFE.

Similarly, the best administrators begin each day with a T.G.I.T. (Thank Goodness It's Today) attitude. They wake up with a feeling of gratitude because they are above ground and not listed in the obituary column. They walk the walk and talk the talk with a personal mission of, "This is my day and NO ONE IS GOING TO TAKE IT FROM ME OR RUIN IT."

They enter the building with style, confidence, and a willingness to deal with all situations calmly, professionally, fairly, and happily. (YES, happily!)

Even throughout the most negative of situations, the best administrators have shared that to maintain a positive attitude, they focus on four major thoughts:

(1) How fortunate they are that they have the skills to deal with this situation professionally, even if they don't (they fake it until they make it);

(2) How grateful they are for their profession and the ability to make a difference in the lives of students (you MUST go to school—you're the PRINCIPAL);

(3) The best strategy to ensure a win/win outcome (wet noodle whipping is NOT an option); and

(4) How excited they will be when this encounter is over so they can move on to the next learning experience.

In all seriousness, success is based on attitude. One then might question, "How do you obtain the ability to maintain a positive attitude on a daily basis and practice the cheerleader-leader style espoused by Guy Bennett?" The answer: it takes a special person who is willing to "C's" (and seize) the day (carpe diem) through C-ommitment, C-onviction, C-haracter, C-onsistency, and C-onnectedness.

C-OMMITMENT

We have all heard the scenario concerning an egg and bacon breakfast. In assessing those involved, we know that the difference is that the chicken was only a contributor, whereas the pig was committed. The same goes for great administrators—they are fully committed to do whatever it takes to support staff, students, parents, and the community. They embark upon each day with a "go above and beyond" attitude. They have a "Rocky" approach to the challenges, choices, and dealings of every day. They WILL make it to the top despite all of the obstacles.

Obviously, not everyone else will always have the same attitude, but that doesn't matter. Great leaders continually make decisions based on what is best for all the people involved.

C-ONVICTION

Great administrators have conviction. They have a personal mission statement that they abide by every day. Being a leader who innovates, involves all, trusts, and does the right thing is the foundation of their existence. Because of their conviction, great administrators live and breathe a FERVOR that permeates the building. Their pride for the profession is demonstrated throughout the community.

C-HARACTER

The definition of character is an individual's pattern of behavior or personality or the traits that define who they are. This means our character is defined by our actions and develops over time. Great leaders demonstrate integrity and model a code of ethics admired by all. Respect, honesty, and spirit are attributes that attract success. Especially spirit—that excitement and enthusiasm that makes a team want to be and do their very best.

A person with strong character shows determination, energy, discipline, strength of will, and guts.

C-ONSISTENCY

One of the most difficult attributes of a great administrator is consistency. So many variables can determine how one handles a situation. It is the react vs. respond model. However, great administrators work diligently to RESPOND consistently and never over-REACT. I truly believe that the best teacher NEVER forgets what it is like to be a student and the best administrator NEVER forgets what it is like to be a teacher.

C-ONNECTEDNESS

Outstanding leaders work effortlessly to ensure that a sense of connectedness exists for all who choose to be involved. They make sure that everyone feels a part of the mission, school, and success. Celebrations and opportunities for recognitions are ongoing. In "connected" schools, people have fun, compliment one another, socialize, take care of one another, and make certain that communication is ongoing and positive. A "connected" school is a "people-oriented" school.

We have heard, "It's not your aptitude but your attitude that determines your altitude." An attitude of gratitude is essential to pave the way toward excellence and a winning personality.

PLEASING PERSONALITY

When educators are asked what makes their administrator so great, many begin by saying he/she is a wonderful human being. Humanness is so essential in dealing with the business of education and its many challenges. A leader with a pleasing personality is one who not only displays intelligence and confidence, but also dresses for success. Your total personality is determined by your appearance, your actions, your attitude, and your answers.

A confident leader talks clearly and convincingly about who they are and where they are going. They truly care about others, take time to smile and greet people using names, and are seldom heard using the word "I." They thrive in a climate of candor and are recognized as inspiring coaches who motivate and influence others.

◆ ◆ ◆

"Coaching is unlocking a person's potential to maximize their own performance. It is helping them to learn rather than teaching them."
–John Whitmore

◆ ◆ ◆

PASSION

Bernard de Fontenelle stated that passion is "the winds necessary to put everything in motion, though they often cause storms." The best leaders absolutely LOVE what they do and have a fire in their belly for the joy they experience in working. Exuberant leaders emit an eagerness and excitement that is contagious. They have the commitment and conviction that others admire and respect.

Leaders with passion set examples, pave new roads, and light fires. They help others realize their talents and strengths. Within minutes of visiting a school for the first time, one can identify the existence or absence of passionate leaders by watching and talking to the other adults and students in the building. The most effective leaders put their HEART into their career. Staff members easily concur that HEART-felt administrators:

• H —— Hear and respect me.

• E —— Encourage me to do and be my best.

• A —— Applaud and appreciate my efforts and successes.

• R —— Respond, not REACT to all situations.

• T —— Trust my decisions, beliefs, and professionalism.

Passion is like a fine dining experience—it is difficult to define, but you know when you have had one.

PURPOSE

Without purpose one has no direction. Consequently, the finest leaders begin with their personal mission that basically comes from the heart. They take the time to ponder who they are, why they do what they do, what they want to become, where they are going and how they will get there. It does not have to be a formalized and detailed statement, just reflection. My own personal daily mission is reflected in the following:

• I will begin the day with the Thank Goodness It's Today (T.G.I.T.) philosophy.

• I will think: "This is my day and no one is going to ruin it for me."

• I will be as cheerful and friendly as possible.

• I will be less critical and more tolerant of my students and my colleagues.

• I will be the BEST I can be.

• I will remember what it was like to be a student.

• I will try to maintain a POSITIVE ATTITUDE throughout the day and in all circumstances.

• I will "seek first to UNDERSTAND and then to be UNDERSTOOD."

• I will not worry or complain about that which I cannot control.

• I will deal with all situations calmly.

• I will share my smile at least five times.

Once a leader has a directed personal mission they may want to share it with the staff. They can then work with their faculty to develop a school-wide mission and vision that drives the motives of everyone in the school.

In discussing mission and vision, we must first clarify the differences between these terms. There is a clear distinction between the two and they are sometimes wrongly addressed as analogous. The most perceptive leaders know that the mission is the purpose or reason for being, and a direction (not a destination). It provides the foundation for a staff. The vision is the future one seeks to create. These two terms are related, revolving around students, but have distinguishing functions. The essence of great leadership is working with a staff to concisely define their mission (or leading star) and their vision (or long-term purpose).

MISSION

A mission must be what everyone truly believes and can articulate. I find it humorous when a staff spends a great deal of time developing a mission statement, coming to a consensus, having the statement printed on business cards, stationary, and posters and yet, when a visitor enters the building and asks what their mission is, everyone scurries to find where it is written. A mission statement must be felt in the heart and addressed every day. Every act occurs with the mission statement as the principle driving influence. It can be as simplistic yet as powerful as "Connors Middle School—Where the BEST GET BETTER," or "Sneller Middle School—Where EVERYBODY is SOMEBODY." It describes the purpose that motivates the adults to show up to work daily. And, most importantly, it has value, significance, and is unhesitatingly expressed by all without reference to a handbook or cheat sheet.

VISION

In addressing vision, I recall Helen Keller's response to a person who said, "I can't imagine being blind, there can't be anything worse." Helen replied, "I can—being sighted with NO VISION." How true.

Effective administrators work with the staff in translating the mission into a compelling vision or meaningful intended results. Through the involvement of all, they develop detailed plans on where they want to be in the next five years. They identify potential barriers, setbacks, and bumps in the road. They assess available resources and team players. They address the following questions:

- What are we here for?

- What is the present situation?

- Are we where we want to be?

- How can we better meet the needs of ALL the students?

- What is our vision as a faculty?

- What do we need to change to get closer to our overall vision?

- How can these changes be made?

- What resources do we need to be successful?

- How can we involve all in being successful?

- What are the major setbacks?

- What are the solutions?

- How do we measure success?

Remember, it wasn't raining when Noah built the ark!

Once a vision is defined, the leader and staff ensures all key decisions and plans relate back to the mission statement. Also, the best leaders appreciate the fact that the mission and vision statements must be re-examined continuously and are always changing. As Warren Bennis says, "Vision animates, inspires, and transforms purpose into action."

PATIENCE

The best definition of patience is by John Ciardi who said, "Patience is the ability to CARE slowly." Leaders realize they cannot be supermen/women. They can only do so much and through patience they take "baby steps" and have a supportive network to assist.

Patience is a virtue and a necessary one to be a 21st century leader.

I once worked in a restaurant with a very temperamental chef. His philosophy was "management by throwing BLUNT INSTRUMENTS." When angry he had a tendency to REACT and throw whatever was in his hand—and many times it was a cleaver. He never cut anyone, but sure scared many. Obviously, patience was not in his vocabulary. Confident leaders have the patience to wait for success. They profess a style of management by caring, sharing, and daring.

PERSISTENCE

Persistence is the mother of success. The best administrators have a "never give up" attitude and finish every job they start. They model what they expect of others and if they do not have a skill they work toward obtaining it. Identifying and cultivating talent in others is an ongoing mission. Persistent leaders are relentless in helping others believe in and support the mission and vision of the school. In being persistent, the best leaders focus on the do-able, the conceivable, and the previously unthinkable.

PEOPLE-ORIENTED

As an educator, one MUST like people to be successful. It is a people-focused partnership that requires a mastery of human relations skills. The best administrators enjoy being around adults and students. They spend an intense amount of time on developing, improving, refining, and investing in relationships. They represent the ambassadors of the system.

The best administrators exhibit an attitude of care and compassion for those in need. Additionally, they take the time to recruit and hire the best when possible—knowing, as Theodore Roosevelt believed, "The best leader is the one who has sense enough to pick good people to do what he/she wants done, and self-restraint enough to keep from meddling with them while they do it." When recruiting and hiring are not possible, good leaders invest as many resources as possible into training.

People-oriented administrators have an open door policy while taking time to speak to as many people as possible daily. The way to make people shine is to let them be the gems that they are, and just provide a good setting and a little polish. Consequently, they treat others, as THEY want to be treated. Meaning, the best leaders ask the adults:

• What is the most effective means of communication for you?

• What do you need from me to be successful?

• What are your professional interests/talents?

• What are your strengths?

• What do you believe can make our school more successful?

• How are we successfully meeting the needs of all students?

• What resources/training do you need to improve?

• How can I be a more effective leader?

Continual assessment, involving all parties, is essential. Through motivation, communication, and delegation, extraordinary leaders build a team of successful players.

PREPARED

Just as communication must be a top priority, preparation runs right along with it. An organized and prepared leader is a healthy leader. The more investment you place in preparation, the more you accomplish. Preparation is essential in organizing your day, planning meetings, fulfilling appointments, and dealing with the ongoing interruptions and unexpected occurrences.

Through preparing, effective leaders ensure that tasks and expectations are understood, organized, and achieved. They can make sound and timely decisions and don't get caught in the "management by throwing BLUNT INSTRUMENTS" syndrome. Stephen Covey's book, Put First Things First, is a great resource in learning to be more organized and prepared.

◆ ◆ ◆

"We all sorely complain of the shortness of time, and yet have much
more than we know what to do with. Our lives are either spent in doing
nothing to the purpose, or in doing nothing that we ought to do.
We are always complaining that our days are few,
and yet we act as through there would be no end to them."
–Seneca

◆ ◆ ◆

PRESENT

Administrators who are PRESENT are visible and accessible. Staff members know when he/she will be out of the building. PRESENT administrators are not only THERE in person but also THERE figuratively, which means they know what is going on in the building every day. They can talk about the student body, the curriculum, the teaching staff, and promising practices without taking a breath. They know what the classrooms look like and they take pride in their knowledge of activities. What they don't know, they seek to find out.

PRESENT administrators frequently visit classrooms and do not hesitate to enter a classroom with a closed door. You can tell how many times an administrator has been in the classroom by watching the actions of students and teachers. When a PRESENT administrator enters, everyone looks up, acknowledges, and returns to whatever was occurring. When a NEVER-PRESENT administrator enters, the students begin readjusting themselves while whispering "shhhhhhh," and the teacher stops in mid-sentence or activity and asks, "May I help you?"

PRESENT administrators are in constant interaction with all, look out for people, listen critically, and provide support. They remain open-minded and are soldiers of risk-taking.

PROMPT

One of Woody Allen's most famous lines in a movie is, "Ninety percent of success is simply showing up." Effective administrators create a climate of promptness. They model this quality by starting and ending meetings promptly, informing others of their schedule, and remaining current with trends, research, and practices. With promptness, great administrators also work on consistency and dependability. The best leaders additionally instill in others the need to acquire these essential skills.

PRAISING

EVERYONE wants to be appreciated. The best leaders take the time to FEED their staff by instituting random acts of appreciation continuously. They recognize the efforts of those who do and work with the limitations of those who don't. They encourage adults to display their teaching certificates, awards, and diplomas, applaud individuals for their hard work and take the time to share successes.

Most importantly, however, great leaders provide authentic praise and work effortlessly to implement, maintain, and sustain a positive morale. A school with esprit de corps is a school of highly engaged, energized, and performing adults that are there for the STUDENTS.

When morale is high, students benefit greatly. You can feel the electricity of a highly energized and professional faculty within minutes of entering the building. Great leaders also know the two cardinal rules of leadership:

1. Praise in public, criticize in private.

2. Praise for what's right and train for what's wrong.

Praise that is genuine motivates and activates others to take the time to give small indications of gratitude. Great administrators set the tone for a school that recognizes the contributions of all, and they spend time saying "thank you." For years, I have maintained a having a bad day file (H.A.B.D.F.). You know those days when you awake and go directly to the want ads wondering if the supermarket has openings? On those days, I sit down with my H.A.B.D.F. (which is filled with notes and cards of appreciation from students, parents, and other educators) and begin perusing the messages. Within 15–20 minutes (sometimes sooner, sometimes longer) I realize I am in the right business. Education is in my heart.

A little praise can go a long way and can influence many others.

◆ ◆ ◆

"The mediocre leader tells. The good leader explains.
The superior leader demonstrates. The great leader inspires."
–Buchholz and Roth

◆ ◆ ◆

PROBLEM SOLVERS

As previously indicated, the best administrators spend only 5% of their time on problems and 95% on solutions. It is so easy to sit around and complain about what is not right, what is not working, and how life is bad. It is difficult, however, to identify solutions and put them into action. Great leaders do just that. They believe that failure is not fatal, and they learn from all of life's lessons and experiences.

These leaders have a positive approach to challenges and a network of support to assist when solutions are difficult to uncover. Again, they realize that they cannot do it alone and they invest in the best resource available: the school-wide team. They know that problems are the price of progress and inevitable in the business of school. So stick to the fight when you're hardest hit.

PROCRASTI-BLASTER

The best leaders communicate, communicate, communicate, and ORGANIZE, ORGANIZE, ORGANIZE. Leaders must have control of their time or they begin to sink in the quicksand of PROCRASTINATION. Yes, hardening of the "OUGHT-eries." We have all been there and done that; we know how putting off till tomorrow that which you can do today only leads to STRESS.

As Merrill Douglass stated, "Many people assume that they can probably find many ways to save time. This is an incorrect assumption for it is only when you *focus on spending time that you begin to use your time effectively." Effective leaders manage their calendar, budget, and agenda efficiently and realize the magnitude of weekly and daily planning.*

The type of planner one uses makes no difference. The important issue is to have some type of planning tool to document, plan, and follow through. When successful planning occurs, wasted time is eliminated; one can deal with the unexpected, and discard the CRISIS MODE approach.

PRESSURE PLAYERS

Pressure is synonymous with education. There is not one great leader who has no pressure. Therefore, the best leaders deal eloquently with pressure. They know it is a part of the job. They realize that when everything is running smoothly, SOMETHING IS ON THE WAY. They handle pressure and don't waste their time trying to kill ants with sledgehammers.

To be able to handle the pressures of leadership, the best administrators lead a balanced life where they realize the importance of good health, support, family and friends, and a life outside of education. They take time to energize and self-renew. They realize that how a person deals with conflict and life is determined by personal CHOICE. They choose to respond (healthy) or react/fly off the handle (not healthy). And finally, they don't let the little things get them down. They keep their eyes focused on the big picture. As John Roger and Peter McWilliams declared, "We must learn to tolerate discomfort in order to grow."

Excellence can be attained if you care more than others think is wise, risk more than others think is safe, dream more than others think is practical, and expect more than others think is possible.

PERFORMANCE-BASED

Administrators that focus on purpose and passion persistently look at the performance of all to ensure everyone is focused on a student-centered mission and vision. They spend their time building on strengths and do not FEED mediocrity or the status quo. They take pride in challenging limits and asking the hard questions.

As acknowledged previously, leaders are learners and promote learning at all levels. Thus, conscientious leaders are catalysts with a zeal for life and a resourcefulness that is encouraging. They take on the hard issues and mean "NO" when they verbalize it.

These leaders deal with the non-performers and do not punish the entire team for the faults of a few. Rewarding and recognizing great behavior is unconditional. But unacceptable behavior is challenged and changed. Performance-based administrators are people-, techno-, curriculum-, and budget-savvy.

◆ ◆ ◆

"The purpose of life, after all, is to live it,
to TASTE experience to the utmost, to reach out eagerly
and without fear for newer and richer experiences."
–Eleanor Roosevelt

◆ ◆ ◆

PROACTIVE AND PRODUCTIVE

Leaders with an optimistic and forward-thinking mode are proactive and productive. They demonstrate the out-of-the-box thinking desperately needed for education in the 21st century. These individuals take responsibility seriously and JUST DO IT. They remain "on the edge" and are completers.

The most incisive leaders are confronting and imaginative decision-makers who take charge of their own learning and thinking. Proactive and productive leaders identify major trends and attend as many professional development opportunities as possible. Everything they do connects back to the mission and vision of the school. They live and breathe an "anything is possible" attitude.

PARENT AND PUBLIC MINDED

Last, but definitely not least, are leaders who are parent and public minded. These leaders recognize that it truly does take all of us as partners to produce great schools. The finest leaders do whatever it takes to build a community where parents and other members truly feel invited into the building. They develop a positive public image and are proficient in parent and community relations. The goal is to build a unified neighborhood within and outside of the school.

In summary, great leaders are great role models with a sound purpose, encouraging attitudes, and the "P's" to make sure that everyone who works with them has the following:

- A clear understanding of her/his expectations and professional vision (dreams, wishes, goals, and roles)

- A realization that the most important team is the SCHOOL-WIDE TEAM (together everyone achieves more)

- The ability to be a team player and recognize their role as facilitators and coaches of learning

- The willingness to deal with tough topics and conflicts calmly and professionally

- The opportunities to provide suggestions, ask questions, and be involved in the everyday operation of the building

- A feeling of belonging and worthiness

- An understanding that risk-taking is encouraged

- Personal and professional goals

- A clear understanding that we are here for all students and do not have a "teach the best and shoot the rest" attitude

- *A belief that it is vitally important to connect with parents and community members continually*

- *An understanding that EVERY adult in the building is a role model for students so we must model positive behaviors consistently*

- *A willingness to admit mistakes, learn from them and move on (pessimists look for difficulties in opportunity while optimists look for opportunities in difficulty)*

- *The courage to ask for help while realizing and teaching that "failure is not fatal."*

- *Loyalty to the students, staff, and school*

- *A professional attitude where no student or colleague is EVER "put down" or humiliated*

- *A focus on developing winning relationships*

- *Knowledge of the students and community being served*

- *An understanding that to be successful it is imperative to be flexible with a sense of humor*

◆ ◆ ◆

"The beaver is very skilled at its craft.
It knows exactly what to do to fix a dam.
The last thing it needs is someone on the bank
shouting out dam instructions."

–Author unknown

◆ ◆ ◆

Chapter 5

The M.E.A.L.S. (Meaningful Experiences Affecting Long-term Success) of a Great School

Chapter 5

The M.E.A.L.S.
(Meaningful Experiences Affecting
Long-term Success) of a Great School

◆ ◆ ◆

"The measure of success is not whether
you have a tough problem to deal with,
but whether it's the same problem you had last year."

–John Foster Dulles

◆ ◆ ◆

There are so many variables involved in creating great schools. Leaders who feed their teachers consistently are intensely aware of what needs to be in place to be successful. They work fastidiously to provide meaningful experiences—the M.E.A.L.S—for all adults. They also painstakingly ensure that the needs of students are always in the forefront.

Winning leaders work collaboratively with staff members to provide MANY or ALL of the following: (Again, the subsequent list is a menu of selections compiled through observations, surveys, visitations in great schools, and conversations with the best and brightest.)

- *A STAFF-DEVELOPED STATEMENT OF BELIEFS—A great leader's mission and vision is to motivate great leaders. They ask "What do you believe in?" to everyone involved. From the responses, a statement of beliefs is generated, shared, modeled, and internalized. Exceptional leaders guarantee that the statement of beliefs is visible to all and implemented continuously and consistently.*

- *HAVE FUN AT WORK—What an outstanding concept. The best leaders appreciate the reality that FUN is imperative in building a great school. Extraordinary leaders know that the mission is the vehicle, the vision is the destination, and the beliefs statement is the daily fuel that provides the means. The beliefs define the essence of a staff.*

- *BEGINNINGS AND CLOSURE TO EACH DAY—Too often in schools, the day begins too rapidly with no time for reflection and ends with no closure. In effective schools, administrators begin each day with daily announcements by students, thoughts for the day, and/or other ways to begin on a positive note. Guy Bennett was known for starting each day with a joke of the day from students. They were screened very carefully before being shared, but the students loved hearing their joke and name over the intercom.*

  Closure of the day is equally important. Too often students and teachers are packing up to leave when they see there is 5–7 minutes remaining in the day. At the departure hour, they hurriedly rush from their classrooms and school to begin afternoon activities. Successful schools provide a time at the end of the day for closure to take place.During this time teachers follow through with homework (if only for 10–12 minutes) assignments and necessary materials. Students reflect on the day as they begin to plan for the next day. The goal is to help all students become organized, productive, and successful students.

- *A SAFE AND SECURE ENVIRONMENT—As specified in chapter three, leaders who care about people make certain that all who enter the school building are safe and secure. They consistently ensure that the physical, academic, organizational, and affective environment is people-friendly and protected.*

- *CURRICULUM CONNECTIONS AND PROGRAMS BASED ON THE NEEDS OF STUDENTS—The best schools provide an academic setting that is relevant, current, integrated, and skills based. It is important to remember that without students there would be no schools. Consequently, everything we do must be based upon the physical, intellectual, social, and emotional needs of the students we serve. Ongoing communications must occur between leaders and teachers in order for both to be informed and educated. The most effective leaders believe that curriculum connections are vital and make every effort to provide opportunity for sharing values, beliefs, insights, and goals.*

  Continuous activities tapping into students' potential are also critical. Strong leaders support ways to teach leadership skills and help students develop through clubs and/or extracurricular activities. Personally, one of the best experiences I had as a student was being a member of the Future

Teachers of America Organization. Countless opportunities arose from that encounter. Unfortunately, I have not seen many schools implement similar programs.

- *AN ETHOS OF CARING AND RESPECT—It goes without saying that the importance of providing a caring and respectful ambiance is vital. A caring school is a thoughtful school and leaders who demonstrate a characteristic of "with-it-ness" do whatever it takes to build a caring staff.*

A compassionate and respectful staff cares about each other, the community, and especially the students they serve. Many thoughtful leaders request that faculty members ride a school bus for the entire route of every student that will be attending the school. This practice provides the staff with three lessons:

1. *It better acquaints them with the community and environments in which their students live.*

2. *It provides them with the reality of how long some students are on the bus prior to arriving at school.*

3. *Most importantly, it jogs their memory concerning the comfort factor in riding a school bus.*

As with communication, the importance of an educator's care and concern for their students can not be stated. Students of the 21st century deserve to be connected with adults who cherish their profession and their clients.

- *COLLABORATIVE AND CONSTRUCTIVE COMMITTEES—"Who wants to serve on another committee? No one? Why?" Does this sound familiar? As Henry Cooke said, "A committee can be a group of the unfit, appointed by the unwilling, to do the unnecessary." Unfortunately, one of the complaints in education is the abundance of committees and meetings with little direction and limited outcomes. Successful leaders, even with time limitations and overloaded plates, are sensitive to the number of committees in place, the number of meetings held, and the people serving on the committees.*

In the best schools, everyone is on a committee (preferably ONLY one). The number of committees is decided by the number of staff members to keep the number of committees to a minimum. It is important to also limit the number of members to between 10–12 but preferably 5–7 per committee. It has been said that the duration of a meeting increases with the square of the number of people present.

Once the committees are determined, everything that needs discussion goes under one of the predetermined committees. Meaning, no new committees are ever appointed to avoid committee overload. One of the reasons prompting my departure from the university was my appointment to the chair of the COMMITTEE of COMMITTEES. Isn't that an indication that there are too many committees?!

Typical committees of most schools include curriculum, public relations, student/faculty activities, grants/fund raising, climate, assessment/evaluation, discipline, communication, transition, and technology. For successful committees, purpose and tasks must be clearly defined and resources and TIME to accomplish them must be provided.

An important suggestion related to committee success is to entrust the chair to a non-administrator; and, to provide recognition and appreciation for the chair.. A good chairperson is essential to the management of a successful committee.

Furthermore, the best committees keep brief and concise action summaries and share their agendas with other interested persons. Again, communication of their purpose, plan, and outcomes to their colleagues is of utmost importance.

- RELEVANT PLANNING OPPORTUNITIES—Leaders who do not forget the challenges of their own life as a classroom teacher never overlook the importance of planning. Teachers not only need time to plan during the school day but also a place to plan. If teaming is in place, outstanding leaders do WHATEVER IT TAKES to provide a common planning time for the team along with an individual planning opportunity. Insightful leaders work hard to provide some time for planning during the regular school day.

- WELLNESS PROGRAMS—Superior administrators recognize the need for ongoing wellness programs for faculty and staff. Education is stressful and educators need options to de-stress. One administrator I observed not only had monthly wellness activities and fairs but also had a local masseuse come to the school once a week to get the kinks out of necks and shoulders. Granted, this kind of luxury is not available for most of the schools we know. However, we must take care of our teachers and any way we can connect with positive health practices is highly desirable.

• *SIGNIFICANT MEETINGS*—A teacher once said to me that he hoped he died during a faculty meeting because the transition from the meeting to death would be very subtle. Sad but in many instances unfortunately true. I have personally sat through so many boring, unproductive, and worthless faculty meetings that I could choke. The best leaders meet only when necessary, and they do whatever possible to motivate the staff to be there.

For FACULTY meetings to be effective, the following should transpire:

- *Discussions must take place to determine what constitutes a good meeting. Guidelines can then be developed and followed.*

- *Opportunities for staff members to run the meeting are provided.*

- *An agenda is disseminated prior to the meeting with possibilities for input and comments.*

- *Advance notice is given for meetings, unless an absolute emergency arises.*

- *Specific meeting days are designated and made known to all participants.*

- *The leader remains aware of the fact that everyone has taught all day and very well may be brain dead.*

- *Opportunities to thrash out solutions in discussion groups are provided.*

- *Adults are involved in the meeting—not just read to.*

- *Meetings are held only when necessary.*

- *Door prizes and fun activities/icebreakers are included whenever possible. The goal is to make everyone glad they came to the meeting.*

- *The meeting begins on time, ends on time, and lasts for the least amount of time possible.*

- *A recorder is assigned to be the formal summarizer of the minutes. This role rotates so eventually everyone has the opportunity.*

- *Food is provided to allow everyone to reenergize.*

- *The meeting is focused and guidelines are in place to deal with disruptions.*

- *A verbal summary is provided at the conclusion of the meeting with a discussion of next steps.*

- *A follow-up plan is discussed and implemented with updates provided at following meetings.*

- *The agenda and summary sheet is given to all so they can take their own notes. A sample sheet may look like the following:*

GREATEST SCHOOL ON EARTH FACULTY MEETING

MEETING DATE: _____

MEETING TIME: _____

MEETING PLACE: _____

TEAM/PERSONS RESPONSIBLE FOR SNACKS: _____

TOPICS TO DISCUSS BY:
(DECISIONS MADE, PERSON(S) RESPONSIBLE)

1. Hats Off to: by Mr. Principal

2. New field trip regulations: by Mrs. District Office

3. Upcoming testing schedule: by Ms. Counselor

4. Group discussion topic on lunchroom behavior: by TEAMS

5. Calendar update and events: by team leaders

Again, the best leaders do not advocate a "death by meeting" philosophy. They meet for a purpose and when necessary. They meet regularly with their administrative team and attend team meetings when invited. They also supply the chairpersons of other committees with the tools to be effective. And of course, they do not tolerate inappropriate behavior by the adults during meetings (i.e. grading papers, doing crossword puzzles, reading newspapers, knitting, etc.). All other meetings follow similar guidelines. Again, the most important issue is to avoid the overload of meetings accepting that any meeting worth holding is worth planning.

- *PLEASING ENVIRONMENTS—Leaders who take their job seriously view their school as another home. Consequently, they do their best to offer a pleasing environment starting with the outside appearance of the school. Community members take pride in a facility that is well-kept and easy to look at.*

  Once the landscaping and outside welcome sign is in place, the best leaders continue to make certain that the inside is clean, fresh, appealing, and student-oriented. They strive to do whatever it takes to provide a welcoming cafeteria, a comfortable and clean teachers' lounge, pleasant and clean restroom facilities, and happy hallways. The wise leader walks around the building at least once a week to view it through the eyes of a visitor or student.

- *MEANINGFUL STAFF DEVELOPMENT AND TRAINING—It is obvious that leaders who encourage staff to attend conferences and visit other schools will see rich benefits. In addition, any staff development and training experiences provided on-site or through the district MUST be relevant and practical. The best leaders attend site-based training with their staff to model the importance of lifelong learning. Staff members must be involved in the planning and implementing all staff development experiences.*

- *STROKES, NOT POKES—The best schools are places where there is an atmosphere of random acts of appreciation. Leaders who take the time to thank their staff and show support are winners. See Chapter 7 for a menu of ideas leaders may select from to stroke their staff members.*

- *POSITIVE SCHOOL-WIDE DISCIPLINE STRATEGIES—An entire book could be written on this subject alone. However, it is first important that the discipline plan is positive. Secondly it must be school-wide. Great administrators work enthusiastically with staff members to develop a plan that everyone can commit to and follow. This is not an easy task, but when it is undertaken and achieved, the payback is monumental.*

A school-wide discipline plan must be developed with a focus on appropriate behavior and effective strategies. When the leadership and staff work together in supporting a collaborative plan, behavior improves and there is a decrease in teachers' frustrations. Obviously, this plan is built on the premise that we reward positive behavior. I once worked in a school where one teacher arrived early every day to write out her demerits before the students even arrived. Positive plans are most effective where teachers and teams work together before ever sending a student to the office. Again, the school-wide effort is the key.

- *SCHOOL-WIDE TEAMING—The most perceptive leaders never lose sight of the most important team in the school—the SCHOOL-WIDE TEAM. With a movement of grade level teaming occurring throughout this country, some schools have lost sight of the school-wide team. The best leaders know you can have both grade level teams and school-wide teams. They bring about an atmosphere where everyone feels important and significant. They empower grade level teams while ensuring the school-wide team importance is never impaired. In a school where the school-wide team is foremost, one sees a respect by all for the areas of expertise for individual team members. Every subject area is treated as ACADEMIC and every teacher is appreciated for what she or he teaches. The best school populations recognize all programs and respect all teachers and students. A student was once heard saying, "If art is such a minor subject, why is it the major part of my life?" This point is well taken.*

- *SHARED AND APPLICABLE DUTIES—When you want to learn about a leader, you ask him/her about their agendas, activities, budget, and duty allocations. The most responsive administrators do whatever it takes to hire assistants for tedious duties (hallway, bus, cafeteria, after-school discipline, etc.) when possible. If it is not possible, they work on a rotating and shared duty schedule with the assistance of all. If teams are in place, they assign duties to the teams so there is an equal distribution of duties of this type.*

• *POSITIVE PARENT PROGRAMS AND INVOLVEMENT OPPORTUNITIES—It goes without saying that parent inclusion is essential to the success of a school. Leaders who recognize this meet with a parent advisory group on a regular basis to discuss ways in which parent involvement can be increased. The best schools are parent-friendly and send consistent messages that all parents are requested to be a part of the school community family.*

• *SHADOWING AND EXCHANGE OPPORTUNITIES—Some of the best learning experiences can come from shadowing another teacher or switching classrooms for a week. Administrators who want to provide the most opportunities possible for learning encourage teachers to share with one another and observe effective teaching practices of others on a regular basis.*

• *MENTORING PROGRAMS—Entering a building as a new teacher is terrifying and intimidating especially if it is one's first year of teaching. Therefore, the best leaders have ongoing mentoring programs in place for new teachers to help them learn the system and feel at ease. A mentor can help a fresh teacher learn and grow and become a part of the family. Mentoring needs to be a planned program that is continuous and positive.*

• *TRANSITION PROGRAMS—Discussions must be ongoing within the school as well as from school to school for seamless learning to occur. Leaders who recognize the importance of transition spend time conversing about what students will have in their box of tools upon leaving the school. They also visit feeder schools and spend time with orientation and awareness programs. Opportunities are ongoing for teachers to learn from one another and share promising practices.*

• *INPUT OPPORTUNITIES—Confident and informing administrators continuously request input from all. They share agendas, budgets, and schedules with all for two reasons. First, to keep everyone informed and updated, and secondly to obtain input and suggestions. Administrators cannot do it all alone so they need as much support as possible.*

ALL-YOU-CAN-EAT BUFFETS

Remarkable leaders relentlessly focus on the following. They become so efficient in these areas that teachers can take as much as they please. The buffet table is never bare.

- *COMMUNICATION—Communication is the key to success in schools. An informed faculty is an included faculty. The best leaders communicate one message in as many ways as possible. They put communication webs into practice and use every technology available to get the word out. Weekly communications are consistently followed by updates placed in mailboxes. Simply having a private place to use a phone is critical. Leaders must also be sensitive to different communication styles and ask staff members how they best receive and process information. It is crucial to remember that listening can be one of the most powerful communication tools.*

- *RISK-TAKING—Think of the first person to eat an oyster, now that was a risk-taker! Self-assured leaders model risk taking and encourage it in others. They realize that failure is not fatal and challenges will arise. A staff of risk-takers is a proactive body.*

- *FEEDBACK—Feedback is power. It is the duty of the leadership to provide feedback on a consistent basis. Staff members want to know how they are doing, what they can do to improve, and what is upcoming.*

- *EMPOWERMENT—Keen administrators appreciate the influence of empowerment. Jim Cathcart identifies the 8 "T"s of empowering others as:*

  1. *TARGET: Does s/he understand and accept the purpose or goal?*

  2. *TOOLS: Does s/he have the tools or information needed to do the job?*

  3. *TRAINING: Has there been enough training in how to use the tools well?*

  4. *TIME: Have they had enough time for the training to take effect?*

  5. *TRUTH: Does s/he know how all of this fits together?*

  6. *TRACKING: Am I providing the feedback needed for them to stay on track?*

    7. TOUCH: Is there enough support and encouragement? (The human touch)

    8. TRUST: Do I trust them appropriately for their skill and mastery level?

Empowerment takes time, but when achieved builds strong communities. The most successful administrators believe in empowerment—delegating, entrusting, and enabling others.

• *CELEBRATIONS—Leaders who celebrate provide the vehicle to strengthen and improve morale and raise the success level of schooling. I believe we do not celebrate enough in this business. We spend too much time talking about what is wrong, what doesn't work, and how unappreciated we are. In schools where leaders focus on the efforts and outcomes of talented and committed staff members, great phenomenons occur. Through celebrations achievements are recognized, people are encouraged, and experiences are shared.*

• *SUPPORT—A supportive leader is one who encourages, challenges, and applauds. Staff members want heartfelt support. Like everything else, support begets support. They appreciate an open door policy where concerns and questions are addressed without delay.*

• *95%–5% PHILOSOPHY—Again, the best leaders empower their staff to spend only 5% "quacking" and 95% finding solutions. Solution-oriented people are much more successful and positive.*

• *HUMOR—Humor is an instrument of pleasure. Successful people must laugh and have fun. Effective leaders know that without a sense of humor and enjoyment, the days, weeks, months, and years can be exceptionally long. As discussed previously, a day without laughter is a day without truly living.*

Now that you have surveyed the buffet table, what are the R.E.C.I.P.E.S. (Recognizing Everyone Contributes In Providing Educational Successes) for superior staff morale? A variation of a recipe developed by Marion Payne, a distinguished and outstanding administrator from Baldwin County, Milledgeville, Georgia, includes:

INGREDIENTS:

- *200 pkgs. of daily recognition and respect*
- *200 cans of daily communication*
- *30 cups of opportunities for professional and personal growth*
- *400 cans of humor and smiles*
- *200 pkgs. of daily support and appreciation*
- *100 tbls. of feedback*
- *200 tbls. of wellness*
- *100 tbls. of empowerment*

DIRECTIONS:

As a faculty, mix all of the above together in a large container.
Stir continuously and serve warmly on a daily basis.
Garnish with professionalism and hugs.

Or try this delicious recipe (continued on next page).

ALPHABET SOUP FOR LEADERS

INGREDIENTS:

- *A–ccept and handle responsibility*
- *B–e honest with yourself*
- *C–ommunicate, C–are, and C–elebrate*
- *D–on't let successes go to your head*
- *E–mpower others*
- *F–ocus on solutions and successes*
- *G–ain support from all*
- *H–elp others grow, learn, and improve*
- *I–magine greatness*
- *J–ust DO whatever it takes*
- *K–now your stress signs*
- *L–isten, L–ove, and L–augh*
- *M–otivate yourself and others*

- N–ever forget why you are in the education profession
- O–pen your eyes, ears, mind, heart, and DOOR
- P–rocess information before responding
- Q–uestion, question, question
- R–espect all
- S–trive towards excellence
- T–hink of self as a worthy person
- U–se your talents
- V–isualize success
- W–ork collaboratively and vigorously
- eX–pect challenges and obstacles
- Y–earn to learn
- Z–ap negativity

DIRECTIONS:

Mix all together and serve generous portions daily. Serve warmly.

To summarize, in a school where the leader vigilantly serves the M.E.A.L.S., great occurrences happen for all involved. In a well fed school, a high attendance is predominant, positive attitudes flourish, communication is effortless and ongoing, a sense of ownership is widespread, and community pride is evidenced. **A well-fed school is a respectful school where everybody IS somebody.**

◆ ◆ ◆

"Teachers become more committed and self-managing when schools become true communities freeing principals from the burden of trying to control people . . . The more professionalism is emphasized, the less leadership is needed. The more leadership is emphasized, the less likely it is that professionalism will develop."

–Thomas Sergiovanni

◆ ◆ ◆

Chapter 6

If You Can't Stand the Heat, Get Out of the Kitchen!

◆ ◆ ◆

Chapter 6

If You Can't Stand the Heat,
Get Out of the Kitchen!

◆ ◆ ◆

"What comes out of you when you are squeezed
is what is inside of you."
–Wayne Dyer

◆ ◆ ◆

One of the most meaningful definitions for insanity is doing the same thing over and over again, while expecting differing results. Sound like someone you know? Too often in education, we fail to acknowledge that our game plan is not working. The result: STRESS. As previously stated, there is only one group of people who do not experience stress, and regrettably, they are no longer on this earth. In this business there is much stress, and, as the chapter title states, "If you can't stand the heat, get out of the kitchen." If the stress and pressure is too much for you to deal with, you need to change your MIND, your BEHAVIOR, or your PROFESSION. The choice is yours.

It is estimated that billions of dollars are spent each year for costs relating to absenteeism, turnover, and poor job performance. Ultimately, an increase in burnout and stress negatively impacts our most cherished treasures—children. Administration is a high-stress job, yet the most erudite leaders learn to balance their profession and personal life to avoid ulcers.

What is stress? It is that confusion created when one's mind overrides the body's desire to choke the living daylights out of some jerk who desperately needs it. Or, more professionally, it is the non-specific response of the body to an unpleasant event. Unmanaged STRESS can become DISTRESS, which is unhealthy. Leaders set the tone for dealing with stress. A stressed-out administrator causes stressed-out staff members, who cause stressed-out students, who oftentimes cause stressed-out parents. Consequently, leaders who care about themselves, their staff, and their students make time to talk about stress, find ways to relieve stress, and provide stress-reducing opportunities at all costs.

It is important to recognize indicators of high stress. They include:

- *Dramatic changes in behavior and attitude.*

- *Absenteeism and tardiness.*

- *A negative and QUACKING attitude toward school, colleagues, and any new initiatives.*

- *A confrontational manner in dealing with issues.*

- *A defensive temperament.*

- *A limited interest in getting involved in any activities.*

- *A noted lack of organization and preparation.*

- *A continued physical appearance of tiredness, depression, and unhappiness.*

Astute leaders monitor their own stress levels first while keeping their fingers on the pulse of the staffs' stress level. Stress is a major cause of heart attacks, unhealthy lifestyles, fatigue, tension, and hopelessness. Stress must be managed. Everyone has three choices for dealing with stress in a positive manner. One, we can MODIFY the situation, two, ELIMINATE the situation, or three, LEARN TO BE UNAFFECTED by the situation. If one of the three choices is not put into practice, stress can become detrimental to the success of the person and harmful to other people.

What are some of the sources of stress? Oftentimes, we can become our own worst enemy. Any of the following personal beliefs can contribute to unhealthy levels of stress:

- *I must be perfect and have extremely high standards.*

- *I am afraid to fail.*

- *I am afraid to succeed.*

- *I am not good enough for others.*

- *I am better than everyone else.*

- *I don't have to learn anything else.*

- *I have to do it all myself without the assistance of others.*

- *I don't trust people.*

- *Everyone must love and respect me in order for me to be successful.*

- *I am a loser.*

- *The world is a very bad place filled with very bad people.*

- *I have so much to worry about.*

- *No one appreciates me.*

- *That won't work—it never has and never will.*

- *Kids are just apathetic and uncaring these days.*

This negative self-talk and catastrophic thinking leads to high levels of stress. Positive self-awareness allows one means to deal with problems optimistically and encouragingly. In our business, most stress is caused by problems and challenges. A stress management strategy includes thorough reflection and analysis. A highly-stressed leader might begin by taking some time to consider and respond to the following:

1. *What is my present level of stress?*

2. *What is the primary problem presently causing me anguish?*

3. *How can I clearly and specifically define the problem?*

4. *What are my strengths that can help me solve this problem?*

5. *What have I already attempted to do to solve the problem?*

6. *What is my current attitude towards this problem?*

7. *What changes have to take place for this problem to be solved?*

8. *How can I make those changes (develop a detailed plan)?*

9. *What resources do I need to make the changes and solve the problem?*

10. *What can I do to add creativity, imagination, and humor into my plan for change?*

11. *When will I begin making changes and when will I finish?*

12. *Am I concentrating only 5% on the problem and 95% on the solutions?*

13. *What feedback (personal or from colleagues) do I need to know how I am doing?*

14. *How did I do (evaluate the plan)?*

15. *What is my present level of stress now (re-evaluate)?*

Again, awareness and definition make up 80% of dealing successfully with stress. Once you have developed a plan, implemented solutions, and evaluated results, you are on a de-stressing path. Nevertheless, how many of us know some people who seem to never be stressed? They almost seem SANE. Through observation, conversation, and reading, I have discovered that the S.A.N.E. are Self-disciplined And Nurturing Enthusiasts. They are those educators who touch the future and enjoy their calling. They are that cadre of excited, energized, and student-oriented educators who go above and beyond what is asked of them on a daily basis.

With challenges such as high public scrutiny and undue criticism, societal problems, expectations for educators to be able to solve all of the ills of society and poor parenting, along with lack of resources, inadequate training, never enough time, and overcrowded classrooms and schools, the S.A.N.E. just keep on going. How? BALANCE. Balance in all aspects of life. Observe the S.A.N.E. for a day. You will learn some valuable lessons of life. They are more concerned with BEING than DOING. As Dale Carnegie once said, "If you are not automatically engaged in the process of BECOMING the person you want to be, you are automatically engaged in BECOMING the person you don't want to be." They recognize that results are more notable than sweat.

Through my travels, observations, interpretations, and consultations I have produced a list of strategies fulfilled by the S.A.N.E. Outstanding educators practice these approaches habitually.

STRATEGY 1: THEY REALIZE THAT THEY ARE RESPONSIBLE FOR THEIR OWN STRESS. The choices are in your control, but not the consequences. The S.A.N.E. take time in making choices to avoid additional stress due to outcomes. They don't depend on others to relieve their stress, and they focus on results. As attitude determines the quality of your life. Happiness and fulfillment come only from an attitude of gratitude. What one makes of her/his life is all choice.

STRATEGY 2: THEY REALIZE WHEN THEIR PLATE IS TOO FULL. The S.A.N.E. recognize when it is time to reorganize and change. They learn to say NO, acknowledge signs of burnout, and take steps to avoid overdoing for the sake of their own welfare as well as the welfare of others in their world.

STRATEGY 3: THEY ORGANIZE THEIR TIME AND PRIORITIES. Effectiveness is being in direction rather than motion. Some people always APPEAR busy but when evaluated have accomplished zilch. The S.A.N.E. set goals, formulate purpose, and establish priorities. They know their direction and locus of control. Each day begins with an organized plan by determining five to seven to-dos in priority order. No additional to-dos are accepted until those already established are completed.

STRATEGY 4: THEY LIVE IN THE PRESENT RATHER THAN FOCUSING ON PAST PROBLEMS, MISTAKES, AND/OR GRUDGES. We cannot change the past or predict the future, so it is best to live in the NOW. Yesterday is history, tomorrow's a mystery, today is a gift—that is why it's called the present! Stop and smell the roses. Celebrate life and do not get deluged with negativity. Don't let people who are D.U.C.K.S. (Dependent Upon Criticizing and Killing Success) affect your attitude. Make the most of each day and don't spend time as a victim at a PITY PARTY. Elber Hubbard wrote, "Stagnation is evident when the past seems bigger and more important than the present or future."

STRATEGY 5: THEY FOCUS ON SOLUTIONS RATHER THAN GROVEL IN PROBLEMS. How many of us have ever visited the teacher's lounge and found a D.U.C.K.S.' POND? (Quack, quack, quack!) Unfortunately, some schools have a pond where colleagues endeavor to OUTDO one another with their horror stories, criticisms, and cynical comments. The S.A.N.E. avoid the pond at all costs and strive to be problem solvers—not problem creators.

STRATEGY 6: THEY LOOK CLOSELY IN THE MIRROR FIRST BEFORE JUDGING OTHERS. It takes so little effort to find error with others rather than to re-examine our own existence. The S.A.N.E. are INTRA-spective before criticizing or condemning others. They understand that we all have problems in life and no one truly understands another's until they have walked in that persons' shoes. They know the Jewish teachings that say if we were all asked to sit in a circle and place our biggest problem in the center everyone would be able to comply. Yet, if we were then asked to pick any one of the problems in the middle to undertake, the majority of us would select our very own.

STRATEGY 7: THEY LOOK FOR THE GREATNESS AND ISLANDS OF COMPETENCE IN OTHERS. Every one of us has gifts we have yet to unwrap—revealing talents, abilities, and accomplishments. The S.A.N.E. search to find the gifts in colleagues, students, parents, and others they encounter in life, while unveiling their own gifts.

STRATEGY 8: THEY TAKE RISKS FREELY AND FREQUENTLY TRAVEL OUTSIDE OF THEIR COMFORT ZONE. The only constant in life is CHANGE. Seize onto new ideas and innovations with a zest and willingness to TRY. See the future as exciting and challenging. As Charles Kettering wrote, "We should all be concerned about the future because we have to spend the rest of our lives there."

*STRATEGY 9: THEY TAKE CARE OF THEMSELVES. **No one can work in a profession as difficult and challenging as education and be fulfilled without taking care of her or himself.** It is an extraordinary yet demanding profession. Only the S.A.N.E. survive because they recognize that to be able to work with the whole child, they must respect their whole self. Exercise, friends, spiritual fulfillment, sound financial decisions, and laughter are all involved in BEING. Wise educators never let a day go by without pursuing some form of personal enjoyment.*

STRATEGY 10: THEY LIVE BY A LIST OF NEVERS. The S.A.N.E. don't acquiesce to the old adage "NEVER say NEVER." Their personal and professional missions include character and integrity as a foundation. Consequently, they do believe in NEVERS:

*NEVER say anything to or treat a person in a hurtful or harmful manner.

*NEVER demand someone do something you wouldn't do yourself.

*NEVER put down or humiliate a student or colleague.

*NEVER forget why you are in the business of education.

*NEVER stop learning and improving.

*NEVER forget what it is like to be a student.

*NEVER let a day go by without living, loving, learning, and laughing.

*NEVER forget the list of NEVERS.

STRATEGY 11: THEY RECOGNIZE THE IMPORTANCE OF CREATING A POSITIVE SUCCESS-FOCUSED ENVIRONMENT. The S.A.N.E. create a climate for success where everyone feels as though they belong and uniqueness is celebrated. They do not hide targets, humiliate others, or focus on deficiencies. They define appropriate behavior and believe that the goal in dealing with misbehavior is to get rid of the inappropriate behavior—NOT THE STUDENT. They hold to high expectations while maintaining a caring, compassionate, passionate, and confident persona.

STRATEGY 12: THEY TRULY LOVE THEIR LIFE AND PROFESSION. Some people loathe being around the S.A.N.E. because they appear to DANCE into each day with vigor and vitality while enjoying being a member of the school-wide team. They share the strengths of their school in the community and applaud new innovations. Most importantly, they are active PARTICIPANTS—not spectators—in the game of life.

STRATEGY 13: THEY ARE H.A.P.P.Y. (Having A Pleasing Personality Year-round). The S.A.N.E. have the BEST ATTITUDES, which can be infectious. They are thankful for the job they have and the ABILITY to work. They realize they are members of the most important and influential profession in existence. They make a point of bringing joy into the lives of others.

STRATEGY 14: THEY RECOGNIZE STRESS AND HAVE A SOLID PERSONAL BELIEF SYSTEM. The S.A.N.E. know when it is time to take a hiatus to rest and reflect. They turn stress into success and have a life outside of their profession where they engage in hobbies, physical activities, and DIVERSION. Notably, they recognize stress signs and attentively work on maintaining balance. Their BELIEFS remind them to:

- Show appreciation to others for their actions (you truly do get what you give).

- Take time to tell the people in your life that you love and appreciate them.

- Don't give up and don't give in to negativity—it only increases negative stress.

- Recognize family and friends as treasures and spend quality time with them.

- Keep your eyes and mind open.

- Strive to understand others to better understand life.

- Listen, listen, listen (being a great listener is better than being a great anything).

- Ignore people who are D.U.C.K.S.

- Remember that goals are dreams with deadlines. Never stop dreaming.

S.A.N.E. people are everywhere. They are the folks that make the world a wonderful place. The sharpest administrators work daily to become S.A.N.E. They realize that some days you are the bug, and some days you are the windshield! It is how you DEAL with any situation that will mold your existence.

Additionally, the people we call D.U.C.K.S. are all around. They are in restaurants, airports, grocery stores, and even schools. There are only a small percentage of these people, but their QUACKING is often loud and relentless. They can be heard in faculty meetings "putting down" new ideas. They can be heard in the D.U.C.K.S.' pond making disparaging remarks. They can be overheard in classrooms having QUACK ATTACKS. This is the type of person who, if offered a $20.00 bill from the leader for a great week, will QUACK, "A TWENTY-DOLLAR BILL (quack, quack)! Why can't it be TWO TENS?" (Sound familiar?) So, how does an efficient leader and staff deal with people who are D.U.C.K.S.? Simply:

1. IGNORE THEM. Many times they want attention. By ignoring them, they go to another pond.

2. CONFRONT THEM—"YOU ARE QUACKING." Ask them if they are quacking because they really want change, or because they just like to hear themselves quack. Discuss the negative attitude. Sometimes a professional and confidential awareness discussion works.

3. TRY TO UNDERSTAND WHY THEY QUACK. As Steven Covey teaches, "Seek first to understand and then be understood." Some people are in pain and avoidance. Their negative behavior is a veneer to hide the real issues. As caring professionals, we want to do anything possible to assist others.

4. GIVE THEM A MAJOR TASK/RESPONSIBILITY. Sometimes people who are D.U.C.K.S. have too much time on their hands. They don't feel appreciated and have unused talents. By giving them a major charge they may feel significant and empowered.

5. TALK PRIVATELY WITH THEM TO DEVELOP A POSITIVE PLAN OF ACTION. In severe cases where someone is having a major negative impact on others, a successful leader must take action. Acceptance of continuous quacking will encourage the person to become even more negative. It is the responsibility of the leaders to deal with all issues affecting the climate of the school.

6. OPEN UP DUCK HUNTING SEASON. Give everyone duck calls. When the person begins QUACKING, everyone else can start mimicking him/her with his or her own duck call. This may even cause the major DUCK to laugh.

7. *BEGIN AN "ADOPT A DUCK" PROGRAM. Match the person up with a happy person. When the DUCK is having a quack attack someone requests their adopter to go calm their feathers. The adopter calmly says to the DUCK, "Calm down, it is just a memo about a mandatory workshop, it's not that big of a deal—why don't you take the rest of the year off?" Creating a buddy system DOES help.*

8. *DON'T LET THEM RUIN YOUR DAY. Most importantly, it is your day and you cannot allow anyone to take it from you. Be strong, supportive, and listen to a certain degree. However, at some point you may have to move on and leave the person to paddle on his or her own.*

STRESS is a reality and must be positively dealt with to survive. The finest leaders have appreciation for certain attributes needed to be a stress buster. Many of these traits are discussed in previous chapters. Still, there is one main prerequisite to deal with stress that deserves some further attention. Clearly the most insightful administrators know what we are talking about— A SENSE OF HUMOR.

No one can survive successfully in the business of education without a sense of humor. A sense of humor is imperative to be triumphant as a stress buster. Without humor, stress will eat you up. With humor, the best principals can learn to deal with all situations and learn to lighten up. As with all aspects of climate, the leader sets the tone for the HUMOR quotient of a school.

As everyone knows, the health benefits associated with humor are well accepted. We know that the physiological effects that laughing produces may include:

- *the production of endorphins in the brain*

- *the promotion of deep breathing which sends oxygen into the blood stream*

- *a relaxing of tight muscles*

- *a free face-lift*

- *exercise for the belly (easier than sit-ups)*

- *cleansing of the orifices*

- *a GREAT FEELING*

- *MORE LAUGHTER.*

A sense of humor is:

- *Exhibited in someone who can laugh at her/himself.*

- *Shown when someone who can find something humorous in almost any situation.*

- *Seen when someone can laugh along with others.*

- *Obvious in someone able to tell a joke.*

- *The ability to see the bright side of a hopeless situation.*

- *A "relief valve" in times of tension.*

- *VITAL to be able to "FEED" others.*

To keep focused on the importance of a sense of humor and survive in a challenging profession, the best leaders practice. They take the time to at least attempt as many of the following as possible.

1. *Laugh loudly before getting out of bed in the morning. Start each day off on the right laugh.*

2. *Tell someone something amusing EVERY DAY.*

3. *Smile at least once every hour during the day. Don't feel like smiling? Fake it till you make it.*

4. *Don't wait to laugh. Laugh today.*

5. *Play at least once EVERY DAY and look for fun in your day. If you can't find fun—create it.*

6. HUG someone who needs it most (a non-touching hug such as a smile, a kind word, or a pat on the back will work just as well).

7. Take baby steps. Life is an adventure—not a destination.

8. Maintain a humor log and document the funny incidents that occur. Humor is all around us.

9. Be a WINNER — not a wiener or a whiner. (Do you have enough cheese to go with your whine?)

10. Make HUMOR a HABIT.

Remember, no one has ever died from laughing. A happy school is a "HAPPENING" school. To truly endure, attitude, health, and humor must be a part of your daily life. In concluding this chapter on stress, I would like to leave you with 15 of my personal favorite stress busters that may leave you less stressed and smiling. Enjoy.

1. Write a memo to yourself congratulating "YOU" on being such a great professional.

2. Organize a "hum-a-long." It is difficult to feel stressed when humming.

3. Pop popcorn without putting the lid on.

4. Make a list of things to do that you have already done.

5. Sit down and laugh hysterically at nothing.

6. Send yourself flowers at work and write "from a secret admirer" on the card.

7. Send a colleague a "unique" surprise.

8. Tell at least three jokes to three different people who seem to have a hard time "lightening up."

9. Dream about what you will do on summer break.

10. HUG your boss and thank him or her for a kindness rendered.

11. Page yourself over the intercom and don't disguise your voice.

12. While sitting at your desk, soak your hands in Palmolive.

13. When driving with colleagues in the car, keep your windshield wipers on to keep them "tuned up."

14. Practice making fax and modem noises in the teachers' lounge.

15. Finish all your sentences with the words "in accordance with prophesy."

Go forth and de-stress. You are worth it.

◆ ◆ ◆

"Excellence can be attained if YOU . . .
. . . CARE more than others think is wise.
. . . RISK more than others think is safe.
. . . DREAM more than others think is practical.
. . . EXPECT more than others think is possible."
–Author Unknown

◆ ◆ ◆

FAT-FREE D.E.S.S.E.R.T.S.
(Defining Experiences Structured to Support, Encourage, and Reward Teachers' Spirit)

Chapter 7

FAT-FREE D.E.S.S.E.R.T.S.
(Defining Experiences Structured to Support, Encourage, and Reward Teachers' Spirit)

◆ ◆ ◆

"There are two things people want more than sex and money
. . . recognition and praise."
–Mary Kay Ash

◆ ◆ ◆

Great leaders know the importance of job satisfaction. Employees want to feel appreciated, respected, empowered, and valued. When a leader takes the time to communicate, care, collaborate, and FEED a staff, amazing results occur. A positive leader lets the staff know that efforts are appreciated, failure is not fatal, and recognition through fun is central. These know-how administrators put time into acknowledgment and are applauded for their ability to observe, listen, support, and encourage.

Remember the H.A.B.D.F. I mentioned in Chapter 4? To this day, I maintain my HAVING A BAD DAY FILE. On the days when I want to go back to waitressing or managing a clothing department, I begin by perusing my file. Again, it contains notes of encouragement, thanks, appreciation and love from students, colleagues, administrators, parents, and even strangers. After approximately 10–15 minutes, I realize I am in the correct field—the best profession around. It's the D.E.S.S.E.R.T.S. that keep me motivated.

Influencing other's behavior is difficult. It is a long and tedious process, but change is possible. The most determined leaders do not want to give up on any individual and try as many ways as possible to turn D.U.C.K.S. into E.A.G.L.E.S. (Educators Affecting Growth and Learning for Every Student). Essentially, the preceding chapters or M.E.N.U. of suggestions has led us to the D.E.S.S.E.R.T.S.— the most fun part of any meal. It is critical that the staff of a school is F.E.D. (Fueled Every Day). Jeanette Phillips, a dear friend and exceptional administrator in Fresno, California, models the following D.E.S.S.E.R.T.S. They are presented as a list of options for you to select from— some may be right up your alley while others may not work in your school. The most important goal is to have teacher and staff appreciation an ongoing priority, and NOT JUST ONE WEEK A YEAR. Also, remember—these D.E.S.S.E.R.T.S. are calorie-free and worth all of the effort.

1. FACULTY BIRTHDAY PARTY CELEBRATIONS—Make birthdays meaningful. Don't forget those birthdays on holidays or weekends.

2. SECRET PAL FOR THE YEAR AND/OR HOLIDAYS—Have the staff FEED each other throughout the year. It is best to make sure the gifts are thoughtful and fun, but not costly.

3. "YOU NEED A LAUGH" AWARD—Begin with a tacky gag gift that eventually is circulated through the staff. It is given to someone who is going through a hard time, is stressed out, or is just in need of a smile.

4. "ANOTHER GREAT WEEK" GET-TOGETHERS WITH COFFEE AND SNACKS—End the week with a celebration to share successes and laughs.

5. ORGANIZE DISCUSSION GROUPS TO LOOK FOR SOLUTIONS TO CHALLENGES—When a challenge arises, ask for volunteers to find solutions. Encourage "out of the box" thinking.

6. SUGGESTIONS/QUESTIONS/CONCERNS BOX—Have a central location for a box where staff can leave suggestions, questions, and concerns. Address them in meetings or in written communications.

7. T.G.I.T. REFRESHMENTS AND LUNCHEONS—Thank Goodness It's Today snacks and meals are important. Take the time to reflect and celebrate.

8. SPRUCE UP AND MAINTAIN A PLEASING TEACHERS' LOUNGE—Make the teachers' lounge a pleasing and positive place to be. Get rid of the DUCK pond and encourage a happy environment.

9. *MONTHLY WELLNESS SESSIONS AND UPDATES—Have a wellness committee or a wellness section in weekly communications. Provide the staff with current health information, great recipes, and ways to feel better about themselves.*

10. *"TAKE A TEACHER TO LUNCH", "NO BUS DUTY", AND "RELEASE TIME" COUPONS—Have drawings or randomly hand out "thank you's." Staff members are appreciative any time they can be relieved of a task.*

11. *SWAP CLASSROOMS AND/OR ASSIGNMENTS FOR A DAY OR WEEK—A school-wide team works together and respects everyone. By "walking in another's shoes," staff members learn to admire their colleagues and sometimes realize that the grass is NOT always greener on the other side.*

12. *SHADOW A COLLEAGUE FOR A DAY—In the most professional environments, learning from one another is ongoing. Through shadowing a colleague for a day, while a substitute, administrator, or district-level person covers the class, staff members can learn so much.*

13. *SHADOW STUDENTS FOR A DAY—One of the best learning tools is to become a student through the day by shadowing. Again, having the class covered by a substitute, administrator, or district-level person enhances the experience for all.*

14. *PAT-ON-THE-BACK BULLETIN BOARD—Have a place for the staff where success and accomplishments are acknowledged. For example, this is the perfect place to congratulate a colleague whose child has just graduated from college.*

15. *DRESS DIFFERENTLY DAY (BACKWARDS, HATS, LIKE THE STUDENTS, ETC.)—Do whatever it takes for the students to see that the adults in the school are human. Have fun.*

16. *PRINCIPAL FOR THE DAY—Through a selection process or random drawing, let a staff member serve as principal for the day once a month or week. It's amazing how much respect the administration will receive following the exchange. The administrator, in turn, takes the staff member's class for the day.*

17. *TEACHERS OF THE MONTH—This can only work in a highly professional school with an esprit de corp. A group of students are the "judges" and select the teachers each month. The selected teachers are interviewed, photographed, and spoiled for the month.*

18. *"HATS OFF TO YOU" AWARD—Design a tacky/fun hat that is given to a staff member to recognize an accomplishment. She/he has to wear it for the day.*

19. *DESIGN A FACULTY COOKBOOK—This is a great fund-raiser to finance all of these suggested activities. Have the staff and possibly parents/students share their favorite recipes.*

20. *ORGANIZE BOOK TALKS OR JOURNAL DISCUSSIONS—We all want to read and know more. A great way to connect, grow, and share is through a book talk group where a recent book or journal is discussed. This can be a fun way to learn and get together once a month or every other month.*

21. *SCHOOL-WIDE E-MAIL AND VOICE MAIL—Again, techno-savvy leaders want techno-savvy staff members. Work vigorously to put in place as many means of communication as possible.*

22. *HAVE A "WHINE AND CHEESE" PARTY—Do you have a stressed-out staff going through major changes? Bring everyone together and let them WHINE or QUACK with some cheese and drinks. Whining and quacking are okay as long as 95% of the time, after quaking and whining is finished, is spent on solutions.*

23. *"ADOPT-A-STAFF-MEMBER" PROGRAM—Have parents and community members adopt a member of the staff. Their goal is to show gratitude and provide the staff member with perks throughout the year. Obviously, for this program to work, EVERY staff member needs to be adopted.*

24. *INVITE A STAFF MEMBER INTO YOUR OFFICE—Leave a note that you would like to see the staff member at a certain time. When she/he enters your office, have a soft drink and snack. Proceed to talk about something you appreciate about her/his performance. Leave enough time for small talk and any questions. Put a positive note in their personnel file.*

25. HAVE A STANDING OVATION—During a faculty meeting, as they walk in the front door, or in the front office—give a worthy staff member a standing ovation. Follow up with a tangible snack or reward.

26. REACH OUT AND TOUCH SOMEONE—Take the time to call a staff member at home on a weekend or at night. Tell them what you appreciate and why.

27. INCLUDE A "ME BAG" ACTIVITY AT THE BEGINNING OF THE SCHOOL YEAR—Take the time to conduct this icebreaker—it can be riveting. Basically, every staff member brings in a bag with 3–5 items from home that they feel introduces them completely. EVERYONE MUST PARTICIPATE and everyone must be given time to prepare. Also, a time limit must be set for the presentation and enough time must be allocated for everyone to present the contents of their bags. If the activity will take more than a day, a random drawing of time slots should occur. Staff members will learn so much about their colleagues through this exercise.

28. ARRANGE A FACULTY TALENT SHOW—Again, there are many hidden talents in staff members. Students love seeing the adults in a different role.

29. ORGANIZE A FACULTY/ STUDENT BASKETBALL or VOLLEYBALL GAME—Organize an activity where the students compete against a group of staff members. This can also be a great fund-raiser.

30. HAVE STUDENTS DECORATE THE TEACHERS' LOUNGE WITH BANNERS, STUDENT-MADE SIGNS, AND STREAMERS THAT SHOW TEACHERS HOW MUCH THEY ARE APPRECIATED Letting teachers actually see student appreciation is important. Allow students to organize a celebration.

31. POST-IT™ NOTE THERAPY (I LOVE POST-IT™ NOTES!) — The best therapy can be by writing a quick positive note and slapping it on a desk, coffee cup, or windshield. Easy, fast, cheap, and fun.

32. NAME DIFFERENT AREAS OF THE SCHOOL—Using staff members' names, identify different areas of the building. It can be fun and creative (e.g., The James Gautier Corridor).

33. *PLAN A BRAG AND BREAKFAST SESSION—Invite staff members to breakfast to share personal successes or triumphs by other colleagues.*

34. *PUT TOGETHER A WELLNESS FAIR—Through partnerships and community/parent connections, plan a wellness day/fair for staff members. Plan opportunities for blood work, cholesterol checks, and other exams. Include community resource people who share healthy living techniques. Many a life has been saved through a comprehensive screening at the workplace.*

35. *PLACE A ROSE IN EACH STAFF MEMBER'S MAILBOX—Place a note with the flower saying "This BUD'S for you" and a thank you message.*

36. *DEVELOP A BEAUTIFICATION PROGRAM—Partner with community members and businesses to assist in keeping the facility landscaped and pleasant. Have a parent or student donate a tree, bush, or plant in a staff members' name and conduct a dedication ceremony. Include the media of course.*

37. *INCLUDE DRAWINGS AND DOOR PRIZES AT MEETINGS—Education is an important business, so we must include FUN when possible. Jeff Garthwaite, an outstanding administrator at Warrington Middle School in Pensacola, Florida always has door prizes and freebies at the faculty meetings. He also has puzzles and guessing games where staff members win prizes if they obtain the correct answers.*

38. *MAKE PLANS FOR A STAFF DINNER AND A MOVIE—A great way to learn more about colleagues is to spend an evening with them. A fun restaurant and great movie can be effective. Always remember, however, everyone will not participate and that is okay.*

39. *PLAN A STAFF FIELD TRIP—Surprise a staff at preplanning with a school bus ride. Invite the entire staff to find a seat on the bus and proceed to take them on a ride for the entire route of every student that attends the school. They experience three learnings: 1. Where the students come from, 2. The amount of time some students spend on the bus. 3.The reality of a school bus ride. This activity should be followed by a luncheon in a local restaurant.*

40. *IMPLEMENT A SUSTAINED SILENT READING (S.S.R.) PROGRAM. This program gives staff members an opportunity to catch up on professional reading. It is a program where every day for 15–20 minutes per day at a designated time EVERYONE IN THE BUILDING reads silently. This is a great modeling behavior for students.*

41. *BEGIN A STAFF EXERCISE PROGRAM OR PARTNER WITH A LOCAL SPA/GYM—Wellness is of utmost importance in our field. Any effort to provide a healthy program for staff members is encouraged.*

42. *PROVIDE A SPECIAL PARKING SPOT FOR A FEW STAFF MEMBERS — Through a special program or random drawings, allow the winners to park in a specially designated spot for a week. Put their name on a sign to "reserve" their spot.*

43. *ALLOW A SPECIAL PLANNING DAY FOR EACH STAFF MEMBER — Provide a substitute for each teacher so they can have a full day of on-site planning. This is in addition to district-scheduled planning days.*

44. *PLAN A "WE CAN'T PUTTER OUT" PARTY—When the staff is tired and needs an energizing activity, plan a staff golf tournament at a putt-putt golf facility. Everyone can participate and it rejuvenates the tired.*

45. *ENCOURAGE THE STAFF TO PRESENT AND PUBLISH—Take time to celebrate articles, books, and other items published. Also, recognize any staff members presenting at conferences or workshops.*

46. *PURCHASE A FULL-PAGE ADVERTISEMENT IN THE LOCAL NEWSPAPER—At the beginning of a new school year or ending of one, place a picture of the staff in the paper with a large note of appreciation. This can be even more effective if done by the parents' organization.*

47. *CONTINUOUSLY BUILD A STAFF-DEVELOPED PROFESSIONAL LIBRARY—Make room for a special place for staff members to read and learn. Encourage staff to share materials they want to order and include.*

48. *HAVE A "YOU DESERVE BROWNIE POINTS" ACTIVITY—When someone has done something admirable, surprise him or her with a large BROWNIE and a soft drink. Include a note of thanks.*

49. IMPLEMENT A STRONG PARENT VOLUNTEER PROGRAM—No matter what grade level, parents as volunteers can work if there is an organized program and a commitment. Once again, when parents are partners, the returns are unlimited.

50. PLACE AN APPLE ON EVERY STAFF MEMBERS' DESK OR IN THEIR MAILBOX—Include a note that says, "An apple a day keeps the stress away."

51. HAVE THE ADMINISTRATORS PREPARE AND SERVE A BREAKFAST AND/OR LUNCH TO THE STAFF—This is a LITERAL feeding activity.

52. "CAUGHT YOU DOING SOMETHING GREAT" BOARD—Take pictures of staff members, write notes, or do whatever to acknowledge a team player effort. This works well for students also as a "CAUGHT YOU LEARNING" board.

53. HAVE THE STUDENTS DESIGN SPECIAL APPRECIATION BUTTONS FOR THE STAFF—Students are so creative. Have a club or organization of students that work collaboratively on creating teacher appreciation buttons.

54. HAVE POSITIVE OPENING AND CLOSING ACTIVITIES EVERY DAY. Begin the day on a positive note through "thoughts for the day," "joke of the day," "word of the day," etc. Take the time to end on a positive note with closure activities.

55. DISTRIBUTE HUG COUPONS—If you don't feel comfortable giving real hugs, design a certificate or coupon that says "YOU DESERVE A HUG FOR . . . " and fill in the blank. The staff members can turn in their coupon for an orange juice or snack in the cafeteria or have a drawing each week/month.

56. "BRING YOUR PET TO WORK" DAY—My students used to love hearing about and meeting my pets. It lets students know that teachers are real people. Another fun activity is to have a wall with the pictures of all staff members' pets displayed. Have a "Match the Pet with the Owner" contest.

57. HAVE AN ICE CREAM PARTY WHERE EVERYONE BUILDS THEIR OWN SUNDAE—Have all the makings for a sundae ready when the staff enters a meeting or planning activity. Have a "most creative sundae" contest.

58. PLAN A STAFF RETREAT—*The best dollars spent on growing are through a staff retreat where staff members get away from campus and the classroom to reflect, learn, challenge, and laugh. More successes have come from retreats than site-based staff development.*

59. "YOU DESERVE A BREAK TODAY" LUNCH—*Surprise staff members with lunch ordered from a local restaurant.*

60. WRITE A GRANT OR PARTNER WITH A LOCAL BUSINESS—*Staff members deserve to be 21st century employees. Consequently, they need laptop computers and printers. A technology savvy administrator recognizes the importance of doing anything possible to provide the necessary resources for teachers to be current.*

61. DISTRIBUTE A "WHAT WOULD MAKE YOUR JOB EASIER" FORM—*Have ongoing opportunities for staff members to share needs. However, if you cannot stand the answer, don't ask the question.*

62. MAINTAIN A CURRENT, VISIBLE, CENTRALLY-LOCATED SCHOOL-WIDE CALENDAR OF EVENTS—*A goal is to have no surprises and let everyone know school-wide activities. Ask teams to rotate responsibilities to keep up the calendar.*

63. DON'T EVER HAVE A MEETING WITHOUT FOOD AND SNACKS. —*A simple snack and beverage says "I CARE."*

64. PARTNER WITH A MASSAGE THERAPIST—*Invite a local massage therapist to come to the school once a week with the massage chair. Staff members can sign up prior to the visitation to get the knots out of their necks and backs.*

65. PROVIDE ACCESS TO A PHONE WITH PRIVACY—*As mentioned before, simple access to a phone with a private location is critical. Staff members may have an emergency, a difficult parent call, or a personal need that they do not want to share with others. The ideal situation is to have a phone located in a concealed location for each team or department.*

66. *PROVIDE A PLACE FOR TEACHERS TO PLAN AND MEET WITH PARENTS AND COMMITTEES—Administrators know the importance of planning and having parent conferences. Therefore, the brightest do whatever possible to provide a pleasant surrounding for both.*

67. *ALLOW OFF-CAMPUS LUNCHES—Occasionally being allowed to leave the school for a team lunch rewards staff members. It is amazing how energized staff members feel upon returning.*

68. *MAKE ADEQUATE RESOURCES AND SUPPLIES AVAILABLE — Savoir-faire leaders know that supplies and resources are essential elements in FEEDING staff members. They look closely at budgets, partnerships, grants, and other means of financial support to ensure the staff are not going broke purchasing their own supplies and materials.*

69. *DESIGN A SCHOOL-WIDE LOGO AND MOTTO—F.E.D. staff members have letterhead, pads, posters, pencils, shirts, and other items engraved with the school's logo and motto. On certain days everyone is encouraged to wear the shirts.*

70. *SCHEDULE JEANS DAY—Almost everyone loves to wear jeans. While the BEST leaders model and command a "DRESS FOR SUCCESS" climate by staff members, they are able also to be flexible and allow at least one day a week/month for jeans.*

71. *DESIGN COFFEE MUGS WITH THE SCHOOL LOGO AND THE STAFF MEMBER'S NAME—We all love to see our name. A simple coffee/tea mug bearing the person's name sends a powerful message.*

72. *HAVE STUDENTS WASH TEACHERS' CAR WINDOWS AND LEAVE A NOTE OF APPRECIATION UNDER EACH WINDSHIELD—Students love to be involved. Through a student service club or parent program, take the time to wash the automobile windshields of staff members.*

73. *HAVE PARENTS WRITE POSITIVE NOTES TO THE STAFF—Through communications to parents, encourage them to thank teachers who are deserving.*

74. *INVITE LOCAL PARTNERS/STORES TO DONATE COUPONS TO BE GIVEN TO THE STAFF—Solicit, beg, and plead with local organizations, corporations, and businesses to contribute anything possible to reward staff.*

75. *DISTRIBUTE "GOLDEN ATTITUDE" PINS—When a staff member displays a golden attitude, a shift in attitude, or a new attitude, a simple (not costly) pin is given.*

76. *PLAN AND IMPLEMENT A MINI-CONFERENCE ON-SITE—For a planning day, conduct a staff-developed mini-conference with teachers training teachers. Involve everyone and include some positive media. Powerful.*

77. *ORGANIZE ONGOING MENTORING PROGRAMS—Take the time to prepare for new staff members by developing and implementing an ongoing mentoring/training program. New and first-year teachers feel welcomed and successful when a school staff is engaging.*

78. *PAY FOR MEMBERSHIP/DUES TO PROFESSIONAL ORGANIZATIONS —Anytime we can purchase something to enhance teaching, we all benefit. Attempt to have a special budget for dues and journals.*

79. *HAVE ANNIVERSARY PARTIES—Recognize years of employment for staff members through an anniversary party. Of course, a gag gift is also included.*

80. *REWARD RISK-TAKERS WITH THE "BADGE OF COURAGE"— Encourage and reward coloring outside of the lines. A truly creative leader may even dress as the COWARDLY LION while giving this prize.*

81. *BE SINCERE IN ASKING FOR INPUT—Never ask for input on decisions already made and always share the results of surveys and questionnaires.*

82. *MODEL "CHANGE IS GOOD AND HEALTHY"—A great way to do this is to physically have staff members change classrooms and offices every 5 years. It gives everyone a new perspective plus it FORCES people to throw stuff away.*

83. INSTITUTE A "LIGHTEN UP" BULLETIN BOARD—*This provides a place where everyone can share cartoons, smiles, and jokes (clean of course).*

84. START A "WE CARE" PROGRAM—*Develop a form where staff members can inform the administration that another staff member is experiencing some tough times and needs a HUG or other form of appreciation. Leaders cannot know every little thing that occurs in the building. Therefore, any program in place to provide updates and feedback is essential.*

85. LEAVE A "QUIT QUACKING" JAR IN THE TEACHERS' LOUNGE—*When a staff member is caught quacking, they have to put a certain amount of money in the jar. The money is used for positive incentives and FEEDING.*

86. HOLD A "CAN'T TALK ABOUT EDUCATION" FACULTY GATHERING—*Invite staff members to a gathering where they absolutely CANNOT discuss education, students, and/or administrators. Anyone found discussing these topics must put $1.00 (or another amount) in a basket.*

87. HAND OUT DUCK CALLS TO EVERYONE—*During staff meetings, members can blow on their duck call when unjustified quacking is heard.*

88. INSTIGATE THEME DAYS THROUGHOUT THE YEAR—*Allow the staff to plan fun and creative theme days. Some examples include, laugh day, wink day, resolutions day, and heroes day.*

89. SCHEDULE "WE CAN LICK ANY PROBLEM" DAY—*After a major change or new initiative, invite staff to a meeting. Hand out large lollipops and congratulate them on the successes.*

90. DEVELOP GOLD CARDS—*Partner with local stores and businesses. They agree to give educators a discount when they show their GOLD card.*

91. HAVE A "GO FLY A KITE" AWARD—*For extremely stressed out staff, award them with a kite and the message to take a break and play. Another fun idea is to give every staff member a kite to fly instead of having a meeting.*

92. *ESTABLISH AN "ON A ROLL" PROGRAM* — *This program is for staff actively engaged in trying new innovations. Design a way to encourage attempting new practices.*

93. *PLAN A MAJOR "WE APPRECIATE YOU" DAY FOR THE STAFF BY STUDENTS, ADMINISTRATION, AND PARENTS—A fun banquet (with FOOD) and recognition is always successful, especially when the community is involved.*

94. *PREPARE LUNCHTIME POTLUCKS—Have teams or certain committees oversee and organize occasional potluck lunches. The administration can furnish all of the drinks.*

95. *SCHEDULE SOCIAL EVENTS AT LOCAL RESTAURANTS—Plan a meal function and encourage staff members to attend. Don't get discouraged if some do not show—be pleased with those who do (don't waste your time fertilizing rocks and watering weeds).*

96. *PLACE POSITIVE NOTES IN THE TEACHERS' MAILBOXES AFTER A VISIT OR OBSERVATION—Let the staff know when you have observed a great lesson, an appreciative act, or a student-oriented classroom. REMEMBER—YOU CAN NEVER OVER-COMMUNICATE.*

97. *ORDER BUSINESS CARDS FOR EVERY STAFF MEMBER—Education is a BUSINESS and staff members deserve to have their own business card. This is a great way to begin a new school year.*

98. *PROMOTE THE DISPLAY OF DIPLOMAS, CERTIFICATES, AND AWARDS IN TEACHERS' CLASSROOMS OR ON A "WALL OF FAME" IN THE BUILDING—We are the only business that keeps our certificates, diplomas, and awards in our attics. Encourage staff to let the students and parents know they are worthy of respect.*

99. *HAVE A "HATS OFF TO . . . " SESSION AT EVERY FACULTY MEETING WHERE COLLEAGUES CONGRATULATE THEIR PEERS—Take time at the beginning of every meeting for colleagues to recognize their peers. It takes a mature and professional staff to be able to do this so there is not criticism, cynicism, and quacking. Invite the superintendent and board members to meetings and encourage them to recognize accomplishments.*

100. *HAVE A "GREAT THINGS HAPPENING THIS WEEK" SECTION IN THE MONDAY COMMUNICATION THAT EVERYONE CAN SHARE—Have teachers/teams let everyone know of great activities occurring in the school on a weekly basis. Everyone needs to know when a team or class will be out of the building or a great music performance is happening. Share, share, share.*

101. *REWARD STAFF IN UNEXPECTED WAYS AT UNEXPECTED TIMES—Have fun with recognition and be creative. Have a group run into a staff member's room with confetti, streamers, horns, and snacks when she/he is deserving. Enjoy the moment.*

102. *SEND A CUP OF COFFEE/TEA AND SNACK TO A TEACHER'S ROOM UNEXPECTEDLY WITH AN "APPRECIATIVE" NOTE—Sometimes just a cup of coffee/tea or a soft drink can be worth a million dollars. Take the time to nourish.*

103. *HAVE A "HERE'S CHEERS" AWARD—Give a staff member a bottle of her/his favorite drink with a note telling of something she/he did admirably.*

104. *ALLOW STAFF TO VISIT OTHER SCHOOLS AND IDENTIFY PROMISING PRACTICES—Many times a visitation either validates success already occurring or stimulates creative juices. Plan visitations regularly.*

105. *MAINTAIN A YEARLY STAFF PHOTO ALBUM THAT IS SHARED AT THE END-OF-THE-YEAR CELEBRATION—Give every staff member a "throw away" camera. Encourage fun and creative photos. Put them together to share at the end of the year.*

106. *COVER A TEACHER'S CLASS FOR A PERIOD (PLANNED OR AS A SURPRISE)—Nothing is more valuable than an administrator who takes a class for a teacher (the best administrator NEVER forgets what it is like to be a teacher). This is one activity that is worth a million dollars.*

107. *VISIT CLASSROOMS DAILY AND PRAISE STAFF AND STUDENTS SINCERELY—Be accessible and visible.*

108. *PLACE SWEETS (ESPECIALLY CHOCOLATE) IN EVERYONE'S MAILBOX UNEXPECTEDLY—One of the BEST D.E.S.S.E.R.T.S is chocolate. Plus a surprise is always pleasant.*

109. *INVOLVE THE STAFF IN INTERVIEWING AND HIRING NEW STAFF—Input, input, input. It validates staff.*

110. *HAVE STAFF MEMBERS AND/OR TEAMS ORGANIZE AND CONDUCT FACULTY MEETINGS—The best leaders cannot do it alone. Use the resources in the school constructively. Encourage icebreakers, fun activities, and of course you must have FOOD.*

111. *HAVE ENOUGH COMMITTEES SO EVERY STAFF MEMBER SERVES ON ONLY ONE COMMITTEE EACH YEAR—Don't have too many committees which results in an overload of meetings. Everyone serves on one meaningful, productive committee with a reasonable number of meetings. Someone once said, "Rome didn't build a great empire by meeting—it did it by killing the opposition."*

112. *AVOID CLASSROOM INTERRUPTIONS UNLESS THERE IS AN EMERGENCY—We all know that continuous interruptions throughout a day break the flow. Be sensitive to the intercom and other distractions.*

113. *COMMUNICATE THROUGH WEEKLY NEWSLETTERS, DAILY UPDATES, E-MAIL, TEAMS, AND COMMUNICATION WEBS—Staff members need to know what is going on. Informing leaders start off every week with a one-page update that includes calendar, highlights, updates, "food for thought," and other significant information. Staff members must receive a hard copy along with follow-up by e-mail, voice mail, or other means.*

114. *PROVIDE COMP DAYS AND/OR OTHER PERKS FOR TEACHERS WHO CONTRIBUTE EXTRA TIME AND EFFORT—If possible, comp time is a plus. When staff members go above and beyond, they deserve to be compensated.*

115. *PROVIDE COMPENSATION FOR TEAM LEADERS AND COMMITTEE CHAIRS—Hopefully, a district that recognizes the importance of feeding teachers provides rewards when possible.*

116. *PROVIDE PERSONALIZED NOTE PADS WITH THE SCHOOL MISSION FOR EVERY STAFF MEMBER—The school mission, logo, and motto must be everywhere. Any added perk that the staff receives reminding them of the mission is essential.*

117. *HAVE A "STICKING YOUR NECK OUT FOR KIDS" AWARD THAT CAN BE THE PRESENTATION OF A GIRAFFE (pin, animal, or certificate) AND KIND WORDS*—Recognize any staff member who is a true advocate for a student.

118. *RANDOMLY HAND OUT "POSITIVE-GRAMS" THAT THANK STAFF MEMBERS*—Design and distribute colorful "positive-grams." Staff members and students can also complete them and give them to one another.

119. *ENCOURAGE STAFF MEMBERS TO ATTEND CONFERENCES AND WORKSHOPS, AND ATTEND WITH THEM*—Every opportunity to grow and learn must be encouraged. A staff and their administrator traveling together to and from a conference have developed some of the best initiatives. It is okay to leave the building—especially when you have a competent administrative staff.

120. *INVOLVE THE STAFF IN PLANNING-SITE-BASED STAFF DEVELOPMENT*—Ask the staff for input in planning training. Don't have training just to say you did. Make it relevant.

121. *HAVE A STAFF NEWSLETTER THAT DIFFERENT TEAMS ARE RESPONSIBLE FOR EACH MONTH (INCLUDE FUN INFORMATION!)* —Staff communicating to staff is a plus. Develop a communication piece where fun facts about colleagues are presented and staff members guess who you are talking about. The goal is to unite, communicate, and laugh.

122. *PRODUCE A YEARLY STAFF MANUAL THAT TELLS ABOUT THE STAFF, THEIR BELIEFS, YEARS EXPERIENCE, DEGREES, AND ANY FUN FACTS*—Any manner in which we can communicate how fortunate parents and community to have a particular staff is critical. Let others know how many years of experience your staff represents. Inform them of the different degrees and/or universities represented.

123. *CREATE A STAFF-PRODUCED WEB PAGE THAT KEEPS THE PARENTS, STUDENTS, AND COMMUNITY UPDATED ABOUT THE GREAT STAFF AND THEIR ACCOMPLISHMENTS*—Through websites, staff members can truly communicate goals, expectations, assignments, and needs. Take pride in developing a web page and update it regularly.

124. *GIVE A STAFF MEMBER A "YOU LIGHT UP OUR STUDENTS' LIVES" AWARD—A SPECIAL LIGHT FOR THEIR DESK OR CLASSROOM—Anything a staff member can be given to augment the ambiance of the classroom is appreciated. Ask a local store to donate some lights. Wal-Mart and Target are great partners and supporters of education.*

125. *DEVELOP A POSITIVE RELATIONSHIP WITH THE LOCAL MEDIA TO HIGHLIGHT GREAT ACTIVITIES IN THE NEWSPAPER AND ON THE LOCAL TELEVISION STATION—We MUST be our own public relations advocate in this business. The media rarely comes to us for good information so we MUST go to them. Make the media your friend.*

126. *ENCOURAGE BUSINESS LEADERS, SCHOOL BOARD MEMBERS, AND PARENTS TO SHADOW A TEACHER FOR THE DAY—Invite, invite, invite. Continuously send notes, make calls, and encourage others to visit your school and observe the ongoing impressive activities.*

127. *GIVE EACH STAFF MEMBER HER/HIS BIRTHDAY OFF (OR ONE DAY IF THEIR BIRTHDAY FALLS ON A WEEKEND OR VACATION) AND HAVE A DISTRICT LEADER, ADMINISTRATOR, OR SCHOOL BOARD MEMBER COVER THE CLASS FOR THE DAY—Believe it or not . . . this can be done. What a feather in the cap of the administrator who pulls this off.*

128. *HAVE STUDENTS OR PARENTS GIVE A PLANT AND/OR CARD TO EACH STAFF MEMBER ON HER/HIS BIRTHDAY—Student-run BIRTHDAY CLUBS are an excellent way to get students involved. They can actually plant seeds and raise plants and/or design birthday cards. They love giving a staff member the finished product and wishing special birthday congratulations.*

129. *ORGANIZE A STAFF CRAFT SHOW WHERE STAFF MEMBERS SELL SOMETHING AND THE MONEY GOES TO THE "FEEDING FUND"—A craft show where staff members actually produce the end product is impressive. Many students purchase items solely because they are teacher-designed.*

130. *COORDINATE A LUNCH-BUNCH ACTIVITY WHERE CELEBRATED STUDENTS GET TO EAT LUNCH WITH THEIR TEACHERS. A SPECIAL TABLE WITH A TABLE CLOTH, CENTER PIECE, AND FINE CHINA IS*

USED—Celebrating through eating always works. Make the cafeteria a pleasant place to be where students want to be respectful and use good manners.

131. DELIVER "WORKING OVERTIME" CERTIFICATES THAT EVERYONE CAN PRESENT—A simple certificate given to a staff member recognizing long hours is a win/win. It says, "I know what you have been doing and I appreciate it." All team members should have access to these certificates to give them to their teammates.

132. HAVE A "DESSERTS IS STRESSED SPELLED BACKWARDS" PARTY—Reward staff through a surprise party of just desserts. Take time to share stress-reducing techniques.

133. INCLUDE "YOU ARE A TEAM PLAYER" ACTIVITIES—Hand out a football helmet to a staff member who exhibits the team spirit. Encourage her/him to wear it for the day. Provide snacks throughout the day.

134. IMPLEMENT A PEN-PAL PROGRAM—Reward deserving staff members with a beautiful pen set.

135. ENCOURAGE THE SUPERINTENDENT, DISTRICT PERSONNEL, AND SCHOOL BOARD MEMBERS TO SEND POSITIVE NOTES—Staff members appreciate being recognized by others outside the school.

136. APPLAUD PAY DAY—Place a Pay Day candy bar in everyone's mailbox on the day they are paid. Have a Pay Day celebration.

137. IMPLEMENT A "SURPRISE—YOU WON" ACTIVITY—Tape coupons, gift certificates, other surprises, or money on certain chairs prior to meetings and staff development. At a certain time, encourage all to see if they won.

138. RESPECT THE LIMITED NUMBER OF SCHEDULED PLANNING DAYS—Don't use up the staffs' planning with meaningless activities, and include all in planning any specific activities.

139. HAND OUT "BONUS BUCKS" FOR EXEMPLARY EFFORTS—Design a dollar that you hand out to staff for great doings. Once a month they can use their bucks to bid on items donated by local businesses or staff members. Fun and gag items must be included.

140. *REWARD RISK TAKERS WITH AN OYSTER AWARD AND A DOZEN OYSTERS*—The first person to eat an oyster took a risk. Recognize pioneers with a special award.

141. *INCLUDE T.E.A.M. (Together Everyone Achieves More) REWARDS*—Celebrate the efforts of teams and committees by providing a special lunch or activity. Applaud all team efforts.

142. *SCHEDULE SUPER-STAFF PARTIES*—Invite the staff to bring family members. Make it a family gathering with activities for all.

143. *DESIGN A "WIND BENEATH OUT STUDENTS' WINGS" AWARD*—Give this to staff members who go out on a limb to help needy students. A pin or certificate may be given.

144. *ORGANIZE A SCHOOL-WIDE PLAY/ACTIVITY*—An endeavor that involves everyone can be very positive. A play, dinner theater, or fair gives everyone an opportunity to work together.

145. *HAVE A "PLEASED AS PUNCH" PARTY*—After a group has accomplished something great, throw a punch and cookies party to say thanks. Give each member a little something with the school motto and logo engraved.

146. *ENSURE THAT EVERY TEACHER HAS A CLOCK IN HER/HIS CLASSROOM*—A working clock in the classroom seems trivial but makes a difference. Clean, well-lit, and 21st century classrooms are a must.

147. *BESTOW A "YOU LIT SOME FIRES" AWARD ON A DESERVING MEMBER*—Give a nicely scented candle and note of appreciation to a staff member who motivated a difficult student. Take time to recognize the time and effort spent.

148. *IMPLEMENT A "YOU HELPED ME OUT" AWARD*—The leader gives this award during the first week of school. During every week of the school year, the previous week's winner recognizes someone else. The receiver and the act are published in the staff communication bulletin each Monday.

149. *PLAN SPECIAL ACTIVITIES OF APPRECIATION FOR EACH DAY OF THE WEEK—Through the help of students, plan activities for Magnificent Monday, Terrific Tuesday, Wonderful Wednesday, Thoughtful Thursday, and Fantastic Friday.*

150. *HAVE A "DEVELOP 150 MORE D.E.S.S.E.R.T.S" DAY—Encourage staff to develop and design more and different types of ways to FEED them. Please share.*

When we all work together and take time to care, great things happen. Messages to staff that say "we value you and the job you do" are vital. It is all of us working together that ultimately provides the most positive, uplifting, and safe experience possible for our students. Consequently, it is the responsibility of the entire staff to DEVELOP "FEED THE ADMINISTRATORS," "FEED THE PARENTS," AND "FEED THE STUDENTS" ACTIVITIES. Remember, everyone needs to be fed. The best staffs reciprocate and take time to thank administrators, parents, and students. A F.E.D. staff is conscious of a F.E.D. administration, student body, and community.

In conclusion, take time for D.E.S.S.E.R.T.S. Savor every bite and while digesting embrace the good feeling you experience. And most importantly, always SHARE your D.E.S.S.E.R.T.S. Laugh, love, celebrate, and have fun. Life is short-order D.E.S.S.E.R.T.S. first.

◆ ◆ ◆

"You wouldn't worry about what other people thought
if you realized how seldom they do."
– Eleanor Roosevelt

◆ ◆ ◆

Chapter 8

The Check, Please!

◆ ◆ ◆

CHAPTER 8

The Check, Please!

◆ ◆ ◆

"The purpose of life, after all, is to live it—
to TASTE experiences to the utmost,
to reach out eagerly and without fear for
newer and richer experiences."
–Eleanor Roosevelt

◆ ◆ ◆

And how was your meal? Was it a fast food or fine dining experience? Did it cause introspection or indigestion? Will you come back for more? What are you willing to pay for the experience? Some of you are thinking, "She wants me to do what?" Others are thinking, "She knows me." And of course there's that 10% thinking, "She needs to do a REALITY CHECK." Whatever your thoughts, you must remember that everything shared throughout the MENU is in practice somewhere in this world by outstanding leaders. I wish I could name them all.

In attempting to conclude our dining experience and savor the moment, I would like to conclude with some after-dinner M.I.N.T.S. (Masterful Ideas Needed To Survive). With all due respect to repetition, many of the M.I.N.T.S. have been previously stated. For the GRAND FINALE, review the following as essential to both personal and professional well-being. These M.I.N.T.S. can provide great material for "after-dinner conversations."

1. *TAKE CARE OF YOURSELF. You must be healthy to lead. One of the most neglected aspects of effective leaders is taking care of health and self. In chapter one you were asked to complete a personal self-assessment. Was it difficult? It probably was because in this profession we are taught to be humble. We feel it is arrogant to say something good about ourselves. To take care of yourself, you must be honest with yourself. You can't live your life saying what YOU THINK others want to hear, and doing what YOU THINK others want you to do. YOU MUST BELIEVE IN YOURSELF. I challenge you to return to the self-assessment and try again to be very honest. Life is too short to ignore the mind, body, and spirit.*

2. OVERCOMMUNICATE. Have I communicated enough the need to communicate? After ATTITUDE, I would say the second priority for triumph is communication. Identify all of the ways and means you use to communicate. Discuss this with the faculty and decide if it is working. Be excited about communication.

3. BE KIND. Kindness is the one passport that is time-honored without inquiry. Kindness is the fuel of victory. When you give kindness you receive kindness. A kind educator is a thoughtful educator. Make time for people.

4. ALWAYS FOCUS ON WHAT IS BEST FOR THE STUDENTS—ALL OF THE STUDENTS. Leaders with compassion NEVER let the special interest groups influence their decisions. They are constantly driven by the need to find some success for and a reward for EVERY student. Know your students, support your students, and appreciate your students.

5. REGARD CHANGE AS AN ADVENTURE. Change is synonymous with education. Anyone who cannot handle change needs to find another profession. Most prominently, change happens one conversation at a time. The genuine leaders have the courage to UPSET THE APPLE CART and do not accept the status quo. They deal with the critical mass and, as stated many times previously, do not waste their time fertilizing rocks and watering weeds. Change with PASSION.

6. HAVE A COMPELLING MISSION AND VISION. Everyone must have a purpose. Take time to identify and solidify a mission—personal and professional. Then predict the future by creating it. The powerful and compelling mission statement of the Red Cross is "to serve the most vulnerable." WOW. Years ago, an administrator who said she or he had a vision would be locked up. Today you can't succeed without one. A successful racecar driver without any crashes once replied why he had been so successful by saying, "I focus on the track, NOT on the obstacles I can crash into."

7. VALIDATE IMPORTANCE AND VALUE. Treat others as if they are the most important people in your life at that moment. People want to feel appreciated, validated, and valued. Simple positive gestures can make a great difference in another person's day.

8. *BELIEVE IN AND DEPEND UPON TEAMS. Superior leaders begin with a plan for innovative, supportive, and exciting administrative team. They meet regularly and delegate duties. They focus on the school-wide team and of course grade level teams. Pre-eminent leaders make certain no one is alone or without someone to work with. The attainment of esprit de corp happens only when teams are consistently in place at all levels and everyone is involved.*

9. *BANISH THE BLAME GAME. In education it is easy to blame others for the lack of skills, resources, money, and quality. Stop quacking and find ways to make what you have work for everyone involved. You cannot complain about things you have no control over. Work with feeder schools and have ongoing conversations within your building. Involve the district as much as possible and inundate the superintendent and district level personnel with invites and updates.*

10. *NEVER STOP DREAMING, IMAGINING, AND SOARING WITH THE E.A.G.L.E.S. Without dreamers, imagination, and E.A.G.L.E.S. we would not be where we are in this country today. It has been said that every day we meet future inventors, scientists, and Nobel Prize winners. Unfortunately, we don't know specifically who they are so we must treat everyone as a productive contributor to tomorrow's society. Do not waste a great imagination through worry; dreams with work clothes become reality.*

11. *EMPOWER. When it comes to empowerment a leader needs to remember, "Once you teach a gorilla to dance you have to be ready to dance until the gorilla wants to stop." Empowerment is accomplished by believing in people, not mandates. An empowered staff is a productive and powerful staff. Only the most secure and self-assured leaders empower.*

12. *NEVER STOP LEARNING —LEARN FROM THE GEESE. Leaders are readers and learners. There is so much magnificent information in our world. One can NEVER stop discovering. The lessons from geese are as follows:*

- *AS EACH GOOSE FLAPS ITS WINGS, IT CREATES AN "UPLIFT" FOR THE BIRDS WHO ARE FOLLOWING. BY FLYING IN A "V" FORMATION THE WHOLE FLOCK ADDS 71% MORE FLYING RANGE THAN IF EACH BIRD FLEW ALONE.*

LESSON: People who share a common direction and sense of community can get where they are going MORE quickly and easily because they are traveling on the thrust of one another.

- **WHENEVER A GOOSE FALLS OUT OF FORMATION, IT SUDDENLY FEELS THE DRAG AND RESISTANCE OF TRYING TO FLY ALONE AND QUICKLY GETS BACK INTO FORMATION TO TAKE ADVANTAGE OF THE LIFTING POWER OF THE BIRDS IMMEDIATELY IN FRONT.**

  LESSON: If we have as much sense as a goose, we will join formation with those who are headed where we want to go.

- **WHEN A LEAD GOOSE GETS TIRED, IT ROTATES BACK INTO FORMATION AND ANOTHER GOOSE FLIES AT THE POINT POSITION.**

  LESSON: It pays to take turns doing the hard tasks and sharing leadership—with people, as with geese, interdependent with one another.

- **THE GEESE IN FORMATION HONK FROM BEHIND TO ENCOURAGE THOSE UP FRONT TO KEEP UP THEIR SPEED.**

  LESSON: We need to make sure our honking from behind is encouraging—not something less helpful.

- **WHEN A GOOSE GETS SICK, WOUNDED, OR SHOT, TWO GEESE DROP OUT OF FORMATION AND FOLLOW THEIR FELLOW MEMBER, TO HELP AND PROVIDE PROTECTION. THEY STAY WITH THIS MEMBER OF THE FLOCK UNTIL HE OR SHE EITHER IS ABLE TO FLY AGAIN OR DIES. THEN THEY LAUNCH OUT ON THEIR OWN, WITH ANOTHER FORMATION, OR CATCH UP WITH THEIR OWN FLOCK.**

  LESSON: If we have as much sense as geese, we'll stand by one another like they do.

–Author Unknown

13. *HAVE THOUGHTFUL AND PEOPLE-ORIENTED POLICIES AND PROCEDURES UNDERSTOOD BY ALL. Choice is the food for energy. Every time a policy, rule, or procedure is forced upon others, choice is eliminated. Everyone must be involved in the reasons behind decisions. When people understand the reasoning, they respect the guiding principles. As Alexander Lucia stated, "When you treat people like adults, 95% act like adults."*

14. *SET GOALS. Goals are dreams with deadlines. Whether you want to spend an excessive amount of time or a short period, they are the road maps to success. Take time to design and chart your future.*

15. *UNLEASH TALENTS. Everyone has gold within. Look for that gold and find the gifts of people that can assist in your mission.*

16. *PLAN AND PRESENT MEANINGFUL TRAINING AND STAFF DEVELOPMENT OPPORTUNITIES. Harvey S. Firestone stated, "The growth and development of people is the highest calling of leadership." Everyone wants something that can make him or her better and can be used tomorrow. Successful leaders know that people do not grow and change unless they are familiarized with relevant, practical, and useful guidance.*

17. *TREAT OTHERS AS THEY WANT TO BE TREATED. The best leaders learn about their staff. They find out about others' "stress buttons" and inquire about their needs. Everyone is different and the most adjusted leaders respect others' styles.*

18. *CHOOSE TO HAVE A GREAT DAY AND LIFE. Feeding leaders spin magic everyday. When they want to have a GREAT day, they make one. They are thankful for life and optimistic about the future. To choose this kind of life, consider the following about dogs:*

   - *When loved ones come home, always run to greet them.*

   - *Never pass up the opportunity to go for a joyride.*

   - *Allow the experience of fresh air and the wind in your face to be pure ecstasy.*

   - *When it's in your best interest, practice obedience.*

- *Let others know when they've invaded your territory.*

- *Take naps and stretch before rising.*

- *Run, romp, and play daily.*

- *Thrive on attention and let people touch you.*

- *Avoid biting, when a simple growl will do.*

- *On warm days, stop to lie on your back on the grass.*

- *On hot days, drink lots of water and lay under a shady tree.*

- *When you are happy, dance around and wag your entire body.*

- *No matter how often you are scolded, don't buy into the guilt thing and pout . . . run right back and make friends.*

- *Delight in the simple joy of a long walk.*

- *Eat with gusto and enthusiasm. Stop when you have had enough.*

- *Be loyal.*

- *Never pretend to be something you're not.*

- *If what you want lies buried, dig until you find it.*

- *When someone is having a bad day, be silent, sit close by, and nuzzle gently.*

–Author Unknown

(Thanks to my good friend Dr. Jim Garvin for sharing this lesson.)

19. QUESTION, QUESTION, QUESTION. Questions are the source of all knowledge. Rigorous questioning is like a scavenger hunt. You never know what you will find. Successful leaders must be secure enough not only to ask different questions, but also be ready to respond to challenging inquiries. Always be prepared to "question the question" as Stephen Covey recommends. And, I am sorry, but THERE IS SUCH A THING AS A STUPID QUESTION. So, be prepared to answer professionally (e.g., What time does the 3:00 faculty meeting start?) and with a smile.

20. BE A TECHNO-SAVVY LEADER. Don't ask the school-wide team to be a 21st century staff if you do not model the same. My biggest frustration is with administrators who expect their staff to be technology-literate but say, "I have only ____ years left before I retire, no need for me to learn that stuff." Technology is not a fad . . . it is not going away. Get with the program and get online. Some of the best education related websites include, but are definitely NOT limited to:

- http://www.middleschool.com

- http://www.ed.gov

- http://fdncenter.org

- http://www.aasa.org

- http://www.ascd.org

- http://ww.nassp.org

- http://www.nmsa.org

- http://ww.edel.edu/bateman/acei

- http://www.nsba.org

- http://www.nsprs.org

- http://www.nsdc.org

- http://www.nsba.org/sbot/toolkit

21. HELP OTHERS BECOME GREAT LEADERS. Truly great leaders take as much time as possible to help others become celebrated leaders. Teach others to grab some low-hanging fruit and obtain nourishment. Teams and committees need great leaders that model excellence. Don't be afraid to share the wealth of knowledge and skills.

22. REGARD PARENTS AS PARTNERS. Do whatever it takes to involve, include, and invite parents. Stop making excuses for why you can't—just do it.

23. REMEMBER THE "F" WORDS OF SUCCESSFUL ORGANIZATIONS. We hear the "F" words every day in the best schools. These terms are shouted, practiced, internalized, and modeled:

- FLEXIBILITY
- FREEDOM
- FOCUS
- FAIRNESS
- FORESIGHTFULNESS
- FAMILY
- FEEDBACK
- FORWARD-THINKING
- FUTURE-ORIENTED
- FUN
- FOOD
  (literally and figuratively)

24. CREATE AND TRY NEW R.E.C.I.P.E.S. Do whatever it takes to feel comfortable, be successful, and connect with people. NEVER stop risking and trying. Review the menu and choose what fits with your style.

25. LOVE, LEARN, LIVE, AND LAUGH. Consider this advice from a trapeze artist: "Throw your heart over the bars and your body will follow." The same goes for great leadership. Leaders make or break the success of a school. Be a transforming leader who loves life, learns everyday, lives to the fullest, and laughs.

FINAL FOOD FOR THOUGHT

The common strand that hopefully runs through this entire book is ADMINISTRATION IS A DIFFICULT BUSINESS AND IT TAKES VERY SPECIAL PEOPLE TO PERFORM AND ACHIEVE THE ACTIONS IDENTIFIED. That is why I am presently NOT an administrator. I don't have the qualifications of the HEROES (Humans Effortlessly Revealing Opportunities for Endless Success) who, throughout our universe, are responsible for attaining, maintaining, and sustaining excellence. YOU know who YOU are. Some of you have been mentioned in these pages.

Unfortunately, there is not the time or space to name the millions of other administrators who model many or all of the attributes discussed. CONGRATULATIONS to you for making the most admirable, yet difficult, profession achievable and applaudable. We truly hope that the people in your lives are also pledging to FEED you on a DAILY BASIS.

I would like to leave you with a poem I wrote, entitled *Life is Precious and So Are You*, to use as a mantra for your daily being. Have a GREAT LIFE.

> Your life is what YOU make it,
>   based on the attitude you choose.
> The way YOU deal with EVERY day,
>   tells if you win or lose.
> To win you must be thoughtful,
>   and love all that YOU ARE.
> Appreciate YOUR talents,
>   shoot for YOUR shining star.
>
> Eat well, sleep sound, and exercise,
>   begin each day with prayer.
> Set YOUR course by setting goals,
>   take risks and learn to care.
> Smile, love, give lots of hugs,
>   respect the human race.
> Don't criticize, complain, or whine,
>   maintain a growing pace.
>
> Words like "wish" and "should" and "can't"
>   must NEVER cross your tongue.
> Go for the gold—stretch and try,
>   leave no song unsung.
> For life's too short to waste a day,
>   or live without a plan.
> So THINK and DREAM, don't give up,
>   and ALWAYS say "I CAN!"

◆ ◆ ◆

"If you want 1 year of prosperity, grow GRAIN,
If you want 10 years of prosperity, grow TREES,
If you want 100 years of prosperity, grow PEOPLE."

–Chinese Proverb

◆ ◆ ◆

Do you have some great ideas to FEED your staff?
Please share your recipes.
We would love to hear from you.

Acronyms Used Throughout This Book

C.H.E.F.S.— *Chief Heads Envisioning Future Successes*

D.E.S.S.E.R.T.S.— *Defining Experiences Structured to Support, Encourage, and Reward Teachers' Spirit*

D.U.C.K.S.— *Dependent Upon Criticizing and Killing Success*

E.A.G.L.E.S.— *Educators Affecting Growth and Learning for Every Student*

F.E.D.— *Fueled Every Day*

H.A.B.D.F.— *Having a Bad Day File*

H.A.P.P.Y.— *Having A Pleasing Personality Year-round*

M.E.A.L.S.— *Meaningful Experiences Affecting Long-term Success*

M.I.N.T.S.— *Masterful Ideas Needed To Survive*

R.E.C.I.P.E.S.— *Recognizing Everyone Contributes in Providing Educational Successes*

S.A.N.E.— *Self-disciplined And Nurturing Enthusiasts*

T.G.I.T.— *Thank Goodness It's Today*